101
Veterinary Marketing
QUESTIONS
ANSWERED

Robin Brogdon, MA

AAHA
press

Veterinary Solutions Series
101 Veterinary Marketing Questions Answered
© 2011 by Robin Brogdon, MA

press

American Animal Hospital Association Press
12575 West Bayaud Avenue
Lakewood, Colorado 80228
800/252-2242 or 303/986-2800
press.aahanet.org

ISBN-13: 978-1-58326-156-9

Library of Congress Cataloging-in-Publication Data

Brogdon, Robin.
  101 veterinary marketing questions answered / Robin Brogdon.
     p. ; cm.
  Other title: One hundred one veterinary marketing questions answered
  Other title: One hundred and one veterinary marketing questions answered
  ISBN 978-1-58326-156-9 (pbk. : alk. paper)
  1. Veterinary services—Administration. 2. Marketing—United States. I.
American Animal Hospital Association. II. Title. III. Title: One hundred one
veterinary marketing questions answered. IV. Title: One hundred and one
veterinary marketing questions answered.
  [DNLM: 1. Marketing—organization & administration—United States.
2. Veterinary Medicine—organization & administration—United States. 3.
Hospitals, Animal—United States. SF 756.4]
  SF756.4.B76 2011
  636.089′0688—dc23
                              2011014133

Series design by Erin Johnson Design

Printed in the United States of America

11   12   13 / 1   2   3   4   5   6   7   8   9   10

This book is dedicated to my husband, Tim, for his unwavering support; to my father, Dr. Melvin Kopilnick, a human specialist who introduced me to the world of medicine and compassionate care; and to my dog, Super, whose battle with cancer in 2001 brought me to veterinary medicine and opened doors to a whole new way to be of service to our beloved companion animals, for which I am eternally grateful.

CONTENTS

PREFACE

Marketing as a business tool and a process should not be a mystery. But practice owners and managers often find it challenging to successfully market their services because the intent and methodology behind marketing can easily be misunderstood. The purpose of this book is to simplify and impart the "how-to's" of marketing a veterinary practice. A range of marketing approaches may suit the specific demographics and segments of your business, yet several basic tenets apply to any practice seeking to build a strong foundation and reach a level of profitability that will sustain its ability to deliver quality care.

Veterinary medicine has advanced rapidly over recent decades, and this rate of advancement is expected to continue into the foreseeable future. In addition, changes in technology have enabled individuals to communicate with each other in several ways. Given this pace of growth and change, the whole concept of reaching the pet-owning audience can seem overwhelming as well as expensive. This book attempts to break down the most important steps to take in building an effective marketing plan for veterinary practices and offers insight into how each practice can do so in a way that is authentic and unique to it. Like anything, it has to feel right and resonate from the inside in order to be effective on the outside.

I invite you to take off the old pair of glasses and be open to a new approach that will enable you to deliver veterinary care to more companion animals and their families. After all, isn't that why you embarked on this career in the first place? Seeing positive results in the way of more client visits and greater compliance is what makes this journey exciting. Witnessing the smiles on your clients' faces is even better, not to mention the end result: healthier pets. So buckle up and enjoy the ride—this is supposed to be fun.

1

When it comes to marketing, what is the best way to differentiate our practice from other small-animal practices?

To market what's distinct about your practice, you must first be able to define and clearly articulate what makes it unique. Otherwise, there is no compelling reason for a pet owner to choose your practice over another. A fundamental tenet of successful branding is just that: Develop a core purpose that every member of the team understands and embraces, and that can be communicated clearly to all clients, whether current or prospective. The goal is to become known for something that makes your practice special and to build a system of client service and patient care around it.

Defining your practice's core purpose may sound straightforward, but you will have to distill all that your practice does into one message. The following statement by advertising legend Stavros Cosmopulos helps to illustrate the importance of keeping it simple:

> One way to guarantee failure is to present so many points in your message that none will penetrate. Think for a moment of the Fakirs in India. They can rest comfortably on a bed of nails with many points. They can even fall asleep. Load your message with many points and your audience will fall asleep. But try making just one point in an advertising message, and watch it penetrate.

Resist the temptation to try to serve anyone and everyone. Define and articulate who you want to be, whom you want to serve, and what you want to be known for. These decisions will be fundamental to your practice's success.

How do I compete with nearby low-cost veterinary hospitals that subsidize their low medical service charges with nonmedical services such as boarding, grooming, and day care?

Every practice needs to decide which core services to offer and which segment of the pet-owning audience to target. The adage "You can't be all things to all people" is true, so if you want to serve clientele who are price-sensitive, you need to find a way to differentiate your practice from the ones known as low-cost providers. One way to do this is to clearly demonstrate the value of your services.

Every practice receives calls from "shoppers" who are looking for a particular service based on price. To help convert these shoppers into clients, develop scripts for your staff to use when speaking with such shoppers. This will guide your team to ask the right questions and to deliver information in a value-oriented way that covers what the cost includes. Use the opportunity to establish rapport with the caller by getting his name and the pet's name and using both in the conversation. For instance, "We use the safest anesthesia methods and monitoring equipment so Fluffy will receive the highest standard of care. And there is always someone with Fluffy during recovery so that she will gently awaken from anesthesia on a heated bed and be pretreated with pain medication for comfort. Does this sound like the kind of care you want for Fluffy, Ms. Jones?"

The staff should practice and receive continual training on delivering information to shoppers by phone as well as to clients who are in for a routine wellness check. To take it one step further, offer a telephone shopper the opportunity to stop in for a tour and to meet the team so she can be comfortable with the environment Fluffy will be in for her dental cleaning. Assuring Ms. Jones that you value her comfort level and how Fluffy will be cared for are important considerations and will show how important both client and patient are in your practice.

ⅲ➡ **Do It Now**

Write a sample script for phone shoppers asking about spay and neuter fees. Send it around to members of your team for feedback. Once it's finalized, print it and add it to the training manual for the front-office staff or another procedure manual within easy reach.

How do we effectively market new services?

Before you launch a new service, be sure you have done your research and verified that it is a service your current and prospective clientele wants. It must meet a need that is not being served or is being underserved, and it should have the potential to generate profit for your practice. Then conduct training on this service so that everyone understands its purpose, benefits, and whom it is targeting. Next, together with your team, set goals for the service and implement ways to track its progress in both recommendations and adoption.

Once everyone is trained in how to talk about the service, and goals have been set, begin introducing it to current clients. In the early stages of introducing the service, gauge your clients' interest level and get their feedback to share with other prospective clients. By starting with current clients when you roll out a new service, and by doing so in a measured fashion, you will effectively accommodate the delivery of the service as well as work out any kinks in the process.

Once you feel confident in your team's ability to deliver the service consistently and with quality, you can begin to offer it on a larger scale, perhaps by adding a section on your website with a teaser announcement on your home page. If you regularly advertise in any local community paper, this might be a great place to include the information as well. And if you are participating in any social media, such as Facebook or Twitter, this avenue can help spread the word very quickly.

Don't forget to use your on-hold messaging and invoices as additional ways to introduce or remind clients of the new service. Presumably your practice management software will allow you to customize messages on printed materials. If this is the case, include a one-sentence announcement on the bottom of each invoice. Your reminder system likely has a customizable feature as well, so include this on postcards and email reminders. Finally, consider placing information in the exam rooms to encourage questions and discussion about this service when the technician comes in to gather patient history information. A multipronged approach is usually best for reaching all who would benefit by using the new service.

ⅲ➡ **Do It Now**

Create a list of all means of communicating with your clients so you can ensure that the largest segment of them receive new information in a timely manner and via their preferred communication method (e.g., newsletter, email, text, direct mail, telephone, social media, invoices, reminder cards, brochures, handouts, or advertisements).

How do we cope with so much increased competition from new practices in the area?

One way to manage competition is to deliver such outstanding service on a consistent basis that any new competition's message will virtually go unnoticed. If your clients are loyal, they will not consider going anywhere else, so your first line of defense is to have the very best trained team you can. Satisfied clients sometimes try something new simply for the sake of variety, but if they are bonded to you, that is unlikely to happen.

Next, make sure your clients know you value them at all times of the year, not just at their pet's annual wellness checkup. This means you need to engage in regular communication with a "what's in it for me" message. For instance, if you periodically send out a newsletter, make sure you provide information that pet owners can use, along with references for finding out more about a particular topic. A good example of this would be to share a case study, and then include a few websites where they can learn more about the particular medical condition discussed.

Whether you are using printed materials or electronic communication, make sure copy is professionally written and is complemented with engaging photos. Don't overload your message with too much text. Simple, concise, and clever will capture attention and be remembered.

Engage your team for fresh ideas and develop creative messaging in a manner your clients will relate to. Being on the front line often gives the team insight into the nuances and specific needs of pet owners.

A continuous stream of new clients referred by loyal clients will also help you retain and grow your client base. So make sure the right people are part of your team and that they are delivering the type of service that is sure to generate referrals.

⟼ **Do It Now**

Develop a list of value-oriented information sources that you know pet owners will find helpful, such as why dental health is so critical to your pet's overall health (tied in with dental health month) or holiday hazards (in line with December greetings). Also incorporate case studies or examples where appropriate, as pet owners will relate to others who have actually experienced the scenario presented. Create a calendar for disseminating the information to keep you and your staff on top of regular outbound communication.

How do we maintain and improve our reputation in the community?

Developing and maintaining a positive image in the community require that your community knows who you are and what benefits you provide—in essence, why they should like you. The best way to do this is to be an active part of the community. Find areas of interest to support, both personally and professionally. This is an excellent time to consult your team to help decide where you want to place your efforts. Most people go into veterinary medicine to help animals. As a team, select a few animal-related charities or organizations to serve that have meaning to you and your team. You may even decide to offer your team members a designated amount of time off each year as a benefit to encourage participation in volunteerism. Or you may choose to make a financial contribution up to a specific limit, with the team helping you decide where it should be designated.

To serve the community, you must be out in the community. If you are a patron of the arts, consider an ad in the theater program or serving on the board of directors. If you have children involved in school athletics, consider sponsoring a team. If you are serious about pet care education, think about partnering with the local fire and rescue department to teach cardiopulmonary resuscitation (CPR) and first aid for both humans and pets. The most important aspect of being well thought of in the community is visibility. There is no harm in being seen doing good deeds. In fact, it's excellent business. But most of all, do it because you want to and because you enjoy it. That reaps the most rewards.

What are effective marketing tools in a rural practice?

If your practice is located where the population is more spread out or less dense, you have to look a little harder. Consider what activities are most popular in your area, and go where the people are. Rural populations tend to gravitate to a local main street or common meeting center for goods and services. Schools also tend to be natural places to congregate. Think about establishing a presence at a community center, feed store, local post office, or farmers' market. Work with the local Red Cross to do a blood drive for both humans and pets at the local hospital or medical facility. Offer to teach pet first aid and CPR at the local firehouse where emergency medical technicians (EMTs) can do likewise for humans. Consider partnering with other businesses that serve a similar clientele.

Sometimes the Internet is the best resource for a more rural area, as many people are willing to travel farther to see you. You will need to help those people reach out beyond typical suburban boundaries, and the Web can be the most cost-effective way to do so. To gain access to many people within your surrounding community, make an effort to have a presence on other local area websites that link to your website. Not only will you be visible to those visiting your neighbors' websites, you'll also be increasing your ranking in the search engines by having other sites link to you. In exchange, a community page on your site can give them the same courtesy.

7

In a multiple-hospital situation, should we market each hospital separately or market the whole group?

Don't reinvent the wheel. Unless there is a reason not to market the practices as one hospital with two or several locations, why duplicate your efforts and expenses? Use these multiple locations to your advantage to extend your reach to more potential clients and pet owners by letting them know you have greater resources and conveniently located clinics for better accessibility. If the practices all use the same practice management system, let pet owners know that the advantage of such an arrangement is that they can go to any of the hospitals and their pet's medical records will be available to the staff. You can adjust scheduling of the hospitals' hours so that at least one of them is always open seven days a week; consider extended hours, such as a few late evenings or early morning drop-offs, as well.

Cross-train staff and use the system of economy of scale to take care of bookkeeping, payroll, human resources, and staff development by using one set of resources. This should lower your total expenses and allow the entire team to be more flexible and cover for each other regardless of the location, so long as they are within commuting distance. The other great benefit is that the lower operating expenses should allow for more marketing dollars, and with multiple locations you have more team members to help deliver the message.

How do we develop a unique name, brand, marketing materials, and plan that are not a cookie-cutter application that looks and feels exactly like the practice down the road?

This is a great question and one that, surprisingly, is often overlooked. It is quite common to see a practice named after the founding doctor (Smith Animal Clinic) or a geographical reference (Washington Lane Pet Clinic). This may seem logical, but is generally not recommended, for several reasons. In the short term, the reputation of an individual doctor may help the practice develop a following and build its base of clients. However, it can do the opposite if the owner does not have the best bedside manner. Tying a brand or an identity to one person does not allow the practice to stand on its own and will always be "Dr. Smith's" hospital. That's fine if Dr. Smith wants to be around forever, but in all likelihood, at some time she will want to sell or bring in a partner, and the goodwill associated with the value of the practice can be hard to transfer. In summary, buying a practice with someone else's name attached to it is not always desirable.

A geographical reference in the name may be fine if you never plan to move. That means you have enough physical space and parking to accommodate growth in clientele and services. You then must hope that the neighborhood remains stable in population, demographics, and overall appeal.

Another common theme in practice logos is the veterinary symbol. Many people recognize it, but it is used by so many practices that it may appear generic and unmemorable.

The best way to develop a name, logo, and brand identity is to work with a good marketing firm or designer who can ask the type of questions necessary to help you define who you want to be as a practice. The best designers then translate this into a graphic image that accurately represents you and what you want your practice to be known for, thus avoiding the ordinary or common logo marks and instead showing what makes you unique.

How do I know if it is worth the money to renovate the outside of the practice to improve the look only (nothing functional)?

Regular maintenance is essential to a practice's overall appeal. It is natural to become desensitized to the types of things that pet owners notice when they approach or enter your facility. In fact, it is common for clinic staff to enter through a back door or a door other than where the clients enter, and therefore what they see every day upon entry is different from what clients see. Every day when you open your doors for business, try to prepare as if it were "open house" day, when you put your absolute best foot forward. After all, if it truly is your privilege to be chosen as the health care provider for your clients' pets, then you must act accordingly. Marketing is all about the many individual acts you undertake to create an attitude in the minds of your clients that binds them to you and sustains your practice over time. This compilation of touches, both overt and subconscious, builds a strong brand.

Create a maintenance checklist that is reviewed monthly, quarterly, or annually, depending on the item. This might include the door mats, inside and outside, exterior landscaping, signage and sign illumination, baseboards, countertops, paint, odor, overall clutter or organization, bulletin board, check-out area, art, refreshment area, storage, and accessibility of often-used and stored items. In this manner, you can keep up with regular maintenance and create a small budget for it, tackling repairs as they arise to keep the place looking fresh, attractive, and welcoming.

Ⅲ➡ Do It Now

Create a list of areas in the hospital along with specific items that need regular maintenance. Assign team members responsibility for helping build the list and seeing to it that designated tasks are completed at their assigned intervals.

10

What interior design efforts are best for retaining clients?

Essentially, clients are looking for comfort and function. Because visiting the veterinarian can be stressful for the pet owner as well as for the pet, do whatever you can to create an environment that minimizes anxiety and creates a sense of well-being. Accomplishing this does not need to be expensive. Careful attention should be paid to interior design; enlisting the assistance of a color specialist or space planner can be helpful. Remember, what you are really trying to do is appeal to how clients feel in your practice.

Depending on your practice's goals and vision, you may select colors and art to evoke a particular sentiment, such as calm and tranquillity, modern with bright colors, or homey and cottage-like. Much depends on your geographic location, the building itself, and your personal style. If you are so inclined, music can add a lot to ambiance without being distracting. Give special thought to the materials you display, making sure everything is neat and tidy. Clutter can provoke a sense of claustrophobia regardless of the actual square footage. Complimentary refreshments are always a nice touch, and clean restrooms are a must!

In terms of function, seating should be comfortable yet easy to clean. Be sure to provide a reasonable semblance of privacy for discussing invoices and making payments. If space allows, consider separate waiting areas for cats and dogs.

The best design elements, no matter how subtle, will make clients feel as though you have rolled out the welcome mat in anticipation of their arrival and your focus is on serving their needs. But most of all, have friendly team members welcome each client and pet by name.

11

What should I do when internal marketing training, discussion, and incentives do not work to stimulate staff to buy in to elevating practice income?

If any of your team members do not share your vision for the practice and are not committed to delivering the kind of service and medical care that is important to you, then perhaps it's time to reevaluate your hiring, selection, training, and review process.

Having a mission-driven practice doesn't happen overnight and always involves ongoing training, but it begins with hiring the right people. In evaluating your hiring process, be sure your job descriptions include the behaviors and soft skills necessary for a team member to carry out your vision for the practice. Share the job description during the interview and consider including important attitudinal characteristics in recruitment ads, if you place them. Letting potential candidates know at the beginning what type of person you are looking for and what is required to perform satisfactorily will help some individuals self-select.

In interviews, ask candidates hypothetical or situational questions to gauge their understanding of your mission and core values. For instance, ask open-ended questions that require candidates to think on their feet, such as "Describe a time when you had a conflict with a coworker and how you resolved it with little to no disruption," or "Tell me about an experience with a dissatisfied client for which you remedied the situation and how you turned things around." How well the candidates answer will give you a good benchmark to judge their desire and capability to act in accordance with your values.

Once individuals are hired, it's important that they undergo a thorough orientation and training process so they can actually see how the mission, vision, and core values for the practice are carried out. This process also clarifies what is expected of them with reference to the behaviors they need to exhibit in the course of their jobs. Having a training manual with sample scripts will give employees a good launching point to develop their own styles while being certain to communicate a defined message of the practice.

Motivating the team to perform in accordance with your vision takes time, training, and commitment. Periodically review the mission with your team and have them contribute to the development of systems and processes that align with your vision. Anyone who is not on board at this point may be best suited to work elsewhere.

12

How do we get staff to consistently indicate the referral source to properly monitor marketing results?

Make sure you have a referral question on your new-client form, whether it's online or in print, and train your front-office staff on how to ensure that clients fill in the field. You should be able to create a field in your practice management software system that asks for referral information for every new client. Some software systems will even allow you to make filling in this field mandatory for continuing to the next screen. Just as important is helping your team understand why it is so important to capture the referral source. So often they hear "what" to do, but not "why" to do it. If they have a clear understanding of why and how this information will help the practice determine the effectiveness of its marketing efforts and what that means to the bottom line and overall patient care, they will be more apt to carry out this direction. See also Question 24 for information on how to run a referral report.

It can also be helpful, depending on how much financial information you share, to help your team understand that you have X amount of money for expenses, and the best way to determine how these funds should be allocated is to make decisions based on sound information. It's analogous to prescribing a treatment plan from accurate diagnostic information. Ideally, this will help the team keep in perspective the value of taking the time to gather this information for each new client.

Do It Now

Designate an individual in your practice to be responsible for running a report on a specific date each month containing the sources of new clients. Get accustomed to sharing this information in staff meetings and present what, if any, actions the practice is taking as a result.

13

How do I monitor how our staff is marketing our practice to pet owners on the phone?

Monitoring your staff's ability to market your practice on the telephone, or more precisely, to communicate effectively with callers, depends on how you define marketing. If you are referring to how well your front-office staff converts shoppers to clients (see also Question 15), the results should speak for themselves if you are keeping good records. Tracking actual numbers of callers who become clients, however, is not easy, as it relies on the honor system of the front-office staff because they are who indicate the referral source. But this is an important activity to monitor because every new caller is a potential client. Making certain your team is prepared to satisfy the needs of new callers by providing them information that compels a positive action (scheduling an appointment) is a key step in building a practice.

The best way to convert pet owners who call for information into clients is to train the team, write scripts for as many questions and scenarios as you can think of, and practice, practice, practice. Planning and knowing how and what to say for each type of call will help everyone develop the skill set needed to comfortably discuss the various services you offer and what makes your practice special, and thus increase your client base.

Some practices create incentives for front-office personnel by setting a goal and rewarding them for the number of new clients each month. Even though the front-office cannot be entirely responsible for all new clients, they are the ones who receive the initial calls, which if handled well, ultimately become appointments on the schedule. See Question 23 for the concept of "secret shoppers" to monitor how well your staff does in this area.

⮕ **Do It Now**

Have your team develop a list of callers' most frequently asked questions and develop scripts to answer them. Make time to practice so everyone answering the telephone is comfortable with the information.

14

Where can I find good marketing training videos for staff?

Fortunately, there are great resources today for online training designed for all levels of staff and covering all topics relevant to operating a successful practice. The Veterinary Support Professional Network (VSPN), American Animal Hospital Association (AAHA), VetMedTeam, LifeLearn, Animal Care Technologies (ACT), veterinary teaching hospitals, veterinary technician schools, YouTube, individual practice consultants, and even local or state veterinary medical associations (VMAs) may have resources available. Many are free or can be purchased as a bundle for the benefit of the entire team.

Also, individual animal health care companies, such as practice management software vendors, food and nutrition companies, and insurance providers, produce training videos or webinars. This is by no means a complete list of sources but a great place to start looking, depending on the type of training you need.

Courses with certifications that staff can obtain from the Veterinary Management Institute (VMI), Veterinary Leadership Experience (VLE), and other organizations can help you and your team develop the skills and experience to market your practice successfully. For more hands-on marketing training, consider looking through the directory of VetPartners, an association of veterinary practice consultants, to identify someone who can teach your team techniques that will work to generate business for your practice.

15

How do we get our very busy receptionists to consistently "market" products and services?

To "market" in this context means to convert more telephone shoppers into clients and/or to inform and educate current clients about wellness care or other seemingly elective services. Simply pushing products or services without sincerity will not have a positive, long-lasting effect. But having a similar message delivered or supported by multiple members of the team will demonstrate your practice's true intention and desire for pets to receive the best care possible.

First, determine whether your staffing levels are appropriate for your receptionists to do this. These conversations take time. Staff must have the ability to listen well and be focused without interruption. A good place to start is to review the job description for this position and determine whether it is realistic to expect your front-office team to handle this task effectively. If so, is this detailed in the job description with clearly defined expectations? The size of your team will undoubtedly dictate how much multitasking is required by each role. Have you considered designating a specific person or persons to do this job?

Understanding how booking more appointments and bringing new clients into the practice will affect the practice's revenue and therefore its ability to provide quality care can go a long way toward motivating the team. Incentives can help, too. Consider creating a collective goal for the team to encourage the staff to work together to help build business so more pets get better care.

Staff who handle these types of calls need to be the right people with the right training, who believe that the products and services are in fact important to your clients' pets' overall health.

16

How do we get the doctors who determine the health care protocols to actually follow them? (As an example, after a support staff member has made a recommendation to a client, the doctor tells the client the pet doesn't need it.)

Once again, as is true for so many behavioral standards of a practice, the solution to this problem comes down to philosophy, guidance, and accountability. As the owner of a practice, you have a duty to hire and mentor associate veterinarians who share your vision for the type of care you want your practice to deliver. Many new graduates have an idealistic view of medical care, however, with little practical experience in dealing with pet owners, staff personalities, and managing expenses, and need to be taught how to follow protocols. These protocols should align with your vision but provide some flexibility based on the wishes of clients and the true cost of delivery. An associate who has a broad-based view of care that falls within the guidelines you've established for the practice can be taught how to communicate and deliver care that serves both the practice and the pet. The big "but" is that if you fail to provide adequate training and mentorship, most associates may not meet expectations, may become frustrated, and ultimately may succumb to early career job-hopping, a common occurrence.

The same theory is true for other members of the team. The bottom line is that everyone on your team needs to know how you want the best care to be determined, and then you need to create systems that support delivery of a consistent message and care. Making sure the whole group is working in synch will ensure greater harmony and satisfaction among staff and create more loyal clients who know their pets' health is your primary aspiration. Conversely, not being united in the goals of the practice or how to accomplish them will only fracture your team and confuse your clients.

Do It Now

Develop written medical standards or protocols for all personnel to follow, making interpretation of your vision less subject to individual variations. Delegate portions of these protocols to your medical team and then meet to discuss them and finalize a set of materials that can easily be referenced and followed with proper training.

17

What can the veterinarians do to get out there and market the practice—or should they?

Yes, it's everyone's job to help pet owners understand how your practice can benefit their pet's care. First and foremost, delivering excellent service and care should generate word-of-mouth referrals, especially if you have a referral program your clients know about and if you acknowledge clients who refer others to your practice. See Question 25 for more on encouraging word-of-mouth referrals.

The veterinarian's job description should include an outline of responsibilities, explaining how you expect the veterinarian to participate in the community to enhance awareness of the practice. Being visible and promoting the services of your practice should be an integral part of the job and one that is also evaluated at performance review time.

Take advantage of the individual interests and talents of your associates. For instance, some may enjoy teaching, which would lend itself to speaking engagements at local events or breed clubs, attendance at a pet fair booth, or other participation. Others may prefer working with children and going into schools to offer animal health and welfare programs. Still others may prefer to be less visible. They might contribute by writing articles for your newsletter; providing ideas for your social media outreach; and participating in trap, neuter, release programs or at the local humane society, if your area has such resources.

As a team, and based on the mission of the practice, select a few events in which you want to participate each year, and make it fun by having unique, branded promotional items to give away, if appropriate, or team T-shirts and banners, raffle prizes, or anything else that may attract attention in a positive way. Remember, this is part of serving the community, which involves being part of it.

18

How do I get my veterinarians to recommend more senior screens, dentals, and other services?

The answer to this question has three parts: philosophy, information, and education.

Philosophically, if your practice prides itself on providing the best care possible for each and every patient, then educating clients about the benefits of these services and thus recommending them would come naturally. But even if the philosophy is all about exceptional wellness and preventive care, an effort has to be made to look at each patient and promote these recommendations.

This is where the information part comes in. For instance, you might share with your doctors relevant data on the number of patients you see that could benefit from a senior screening, the number given the recommendation, and finally the number who comply; then show the doctors the same scenario with only a 10 percent increase. They will see that not only will many more patients benefit by this higher level of care, but also it will contribute to overall revenue and profitability of the practice and even their own personal income.

The educational component is all about providing your doctors and staff with the resources and tools to communicate to clients the need for and benefits of wellness care services beyond the basic physical examination and vaccinations. Some practices find it helpful when performing an examination on a patient to have a checklist of all the wellness services a patient may need, depending on species, breed, signalment, age, and so forth. This provides consistency for how doctors approach a patient, and creates a medical standard to ensure that each patient is afforded the benefit of recommended screenings and preventive care that all other pets receive, regardless of the client's perceived ability to pay.

19

We get a lot of new clients coming in every month, but how do we keep them coming back?

As with most service relationships, creating client satisfaction involves many factors, such as skill at asking clients the type of questions that, when answered, will give you the information critical to knowing exactly what needs you must satisfy. But you cannot discount the fact that developing a relationship takes time. As consumers ourselves, we typically divulge information only after we have been made to feel comfortable and that we are speaking with a trustworthy individual who has honorable intentions and can carry them out. See Question 36 for more tips on establishing trust between a veterinarian and client.

Creating a memorable experience for a new client, or any client for that matter, requires that you pay attention to the details. Explain the steps in the process for the first visit so clients have a good idea of what will happen to their pet, how long it might take, and approximately what it will cost. In general, keep the information flowing. No one likes surprises here.

Personalize the experience as much as possible so clients feel valued as individuals, not simply as patient X. Make them feel welcome in the clinic. Use the client's and pet's names in communication and always thank the client for choosing your clinic. And, of course, say that you look forward to seeing them again.

A stable, long-term roster of staff is also very comforting to a pet owner. For clients, seeing the same staff over again conveys the message that your clinic is a good place to work and therefore a good place to bring their pets. And who doesn't enjoy being recognized and acknowledged by name when they visit the clinic? This can happen only if the team remains relatively the same, year after year.

Last, keep doing whatever you are doing that brings in a steady stream of new clients!

20

We recently handed out flyers for clients to participate in a client survey and got only two responses. How do we motivate clients to provide feedback?

Much as with any situation in which you are trying to compel people to do something, your success is greatly predicated on their perception of what's in it for them. Think about it this way: People are busy and don't want to take the time to fill out a survey if they do not see a direct purpose or result that will benefit them or their pets.

Most practices try to keep their surveys short and to the point to encourage participation, but consider trying to motivate clients to provide feedback with different approaches. For instance, if you would like to obtain statistically significant information from your clients in order to make an assessment of service levels or to determine whether there is sufficient interest in launching a new product or service, first explain to prospective survey takers the purpose of the survey and why you are requesting the information. This needs to be followed by a description of how you will use the information and if and when they will be told about the results. If you are asking clients to take the survey in person, delegate this task to the individuals on your team who have good communication skills and have a relationship with the clients. A personal appeal at that level will garner a higher response. It's always a good idea to have an anonymous option as well as one in which respondents can request that they be contacted for additional feedback.

How the questions are written and the survey design should be given equal priority. Try to use the lowest number of questions to elicit the most information possible. A professionally designed questionnaire is sure to add to the success rate.

Last but not least, an incentive may just tip the scales in your favor if respondents will be comfortable providing their contact information. Many will want to remain anonymous, however, so it may not always be a feasible tactic. Providing survey information up front, including how the information will be used, and then following up in a timely manner by sharing the findings and—most important—the subsequent decisions you have made as a result will encourage participation. Ideally, if done well, this will further bond clients to your practice as you will once again prove to come through on a promise—asking for feedback, listening to the results, and taking action because of it. It sure is nice to be heard!

21

What should I put in email newsletters?

If you have done your research and determined that a sizable portion of your clientele would enjoy receiving timely information electronically, an email newsletter can be a very cost-effective and convenient way to communicate all types of information.

Asking busy people to stop and read your newsletter entails delivering information of value to the intended audience. Because people across the generations may have different interests, it is helpful to provide a range of information, from more in-depth educational material to short reminders and acknowledgments. The key is to make the newsletter short enough that it won't feel overwhelming. Create catchy headlines followed by first paragraphs with "read more" links to your website, where cleints can access the entire article. This accomplishes two things. First, it keeps the newsletter brief and allows readers to quickly scan and then read only the articles of interest. Second, it drives people back to your website—always a good thing for exposing them to more of what makes your practice special and reinforcing it as a resource they can count on.

Information pet owners find helpful or interesting includes a calendar of events, pet health care news, an article on an aspect of medical care, breed-specific information, success stories, acknowledgments for referring other clients, special occasions or milestones for patients, and practice team member news. The best way to find out what your clients want to read about is to ask.

Keep in mind that it is also important to ensure your clients' privacy. Publish a privacy statement on your website where clients can sign up to receive electronic communication and put this statement on the newsletter itself. One way to adhere to best practices and spam compliance is to use one of the many inexpensive e-newsletter services. A useful feature of many services is the statistical data available to you as part of your subscription fee. You can track email open rates, links accessed, and more. Having a website and a newsletter is great, and using the information from your visitors can help you make decisions about how to improve upon their experience and really make a difference in your level of service.

22

Is there value in giving away free products or offering discounts to encourage more visits?

Generally speaking, discounting medical services is not advisable and does not result in building a strong client base. Conventional marketing wisdom, backed by many studies, is that the price you charge is the ultimate expression of what you think your product or service is worth. If you discount prices, you're basically telling your clients that the product really isn't worth what you've been charging them all this time, which, of course, triggers a credibility and trust issue. Commodities trade on price. Thus, if you choose to sell your services based on cost, you become a commodity. In addition, discounting is not a sustainable strategy. You will never win a price war. There is always someone who will come in cheaper (e.g., Walmart).

You must know your market well in order to know what motivates your clientele and how they will respond to a discount. Some generalizations, however, can apply to any service-oriented business, as well as one that is most certainly emotionally charged, such as veterinary medicine. A sick pet can trigger feelings of vulnerability in the owner, which can lead to an assumption of pressure to accept a particular recommendation. A better strategy than discounting would be to add more value to a particular service, creating the perception of more for less. For instance, you might add a bath for every two nights of boarding or three free physical therapy sessions with every orthopedic surgery. Value-adds will trump discounts every time!

23

What is the best way to conduct "secret shopper" visits or phone calls to our hospital or other veterinary hospitals?

While you are busy carrying out your duties as doctor or manager, it is natural to want to know how well your team is communicating with clients, as well as how you stack up against the competition. Before you launch any sort of "intelligence gathering" campaign, however, create a list of exactly what you want to learn from the exercise. This will guide you in creating the questions to ask at each clinic, if you will be evaluating more than one, for a proper comparison.

Keep in mind that your approach may need to vary, depending on what you are researching. If you want to compare basic wellness services, such as dentals, spay or neuter, office visit or examination, multiple-pet discounts, and parasite control recommendations, you may find it adequate to communicate by telephone, where you will likely speak with the front-office staff. If you are looking to gather information on more technical treatments, such as advanced diagnostics, outpatient ultrasound, and specialized surgery or procedures, you may find a visit, where you will probably have more contact with the medical team, more appropriate.

To have a secret shopper visit your clinic, ask someone you trust to call and schedule an appointment, posing as a new client looking for a veterinarian. Have the shopper go through the entire process of calling to find out about the practice and scheduling the appointment, listening carefully for the information provided to prepare for his or her pet's first visit. Have the shopper see one of your associate veterinarians and, of course, provide the money to pay for the visit. You want him or her to follow the exact protocol any other new client would. After the visit, give the shopper a form to fill out ranking all areas of service, from ease of scheduling to directions provided, whether a website address was offered to provide more information about the practice before the visit or for downloading and completing forms in advance, friendliness and helpfulness of staff, clinic cleanliness, wait times, whether recommendations were explained clearly, and so on.

This tactic is highly recommended, as nothing beats getting it directly from the horse's mouth!

Do It Now

Create a list of areas you would like to be evaluated by an outsider at your own clinic. Be sure to inform your team that secret shoppers may come in periodically for an unbiased view of how the clinic is doing, with one of the goals being to reward excellent service and identify and improve any gaps that are evident. Then be sure to share results with the team.

24

How important is it to track client referrals and reward clients for referrals?

Tracking the source of all new business is critical. If you don't know where new clients are coming from, you have no idea which business development tactics are working. Because most small businesses have small marketing budgets, word-of-mouth referrals are the most cost-effective way to grow the business. But it is essential that you record the source of every new client so that you can use the data to help you determine proper allocation of your marketing dollars. See Question 12 for more on training receptionists to enter referral sources.

Get in the habit of running a new client source report from your practice management software once a month. Reports can usually be run for any source field (e.g., referrals) or for multiple fields. As an easy reminder, do this at the same time you process and send out your reminder cards. Many of our marketing efforts are not directly measurable, but if you have entered accurate information on new clients into your database, you have an excellent starting place to analyze the effectiveness of your programs.

It's important to reward clients for referring new business, if you want them to keep doing so. Not that people make referrals only when there is something in it for them, but you do catch more flies with honey. And it is always good to acknowledge a referral because it means someone has made the effort to vouch for you, which is a great launching pad to establishing a relationship with a new client that has a lifetime of value.

25

What is the best way to encourage word-of-mouth advertising? And how should you reward those who refer new clients?

The best way to encourage word-of-mouth advertising is to deliver outstanding service on a consistent basis and create a memorable experience for clients and their pets.

It's also a great idea to develop a referral program to let your clients know you are accepting new patients and appreciate referrals. Most important, don't keep this program a secret. At the bottom of each invoice, you might include a sentence such as "Thank you for trusting us with your pet's health. If you know someone who would appreciate the same quality care and service, we are always grateful for referrals." Just like your logo, your referral program should be visible in many locations. For instance, add it to the bottom of your reminder cards, include a message on all invoices, establish a location on your website to thank individuals for referring new clients, mention the referral program in your newsletter, and above all, properly thank those who do refer clients.

As for thanking those who make referrals, you may want to try a few different rewards to see what your clients value most. Don't be afraid to ask them as well. Some clients may like a discount on their next service, and others may prefer an additional service, such as a nail trim, the next time they bring in their pet for an examination. Allowing them to choose between two options is another way to make them feel empowered and valued.

Be sure you roll out the welcome mat in grand style for new clients. If they become fans, you'll keep the new-client pipeline primed.

26

What are some marketing ideas to attract new clients to an established practice in a community where the recession is driving down client numbers and average transaction charge?

As mentioned elsewhere, word-of-mouth referrals are always the preferred way to grow your client base. These individuals arrive at the practice based on the trust of a friend or family member and are expecting to have a positive experience.

Beyond current client referrals, targeting your marketing to specific audiences can work well too. Consider a senior citizen special offering every person 65 or older something free with a visit on Tuesdays (or whatever is your slow day). Then check whether you can advertise this special in a local senior community newsletter.

If it is possible for you to deliver veterinary services to a particular community, you may do even better. There is a large market for mobile services, and if you can reach those who might not be able to get out to obtain care for their pets on a regular basis, you may grow the business without necessarily having to persuade people to choose you over their current provider.

For those who understand that quality health care is important to their pet, but who may not know about you, try aligning with a large company and becoming part of its employee benefit program. For example, some corporations include a pet clinic as a preferred provider, and every employee receives some sort of discount or bonus for choosing that provider.

The same can be done if you happen to be in a location where there is a distinctive population, such as the military. Offer to care for this community with something special and the goodwill will go a long way.

27

What is the best way to get local mailing lists to reach new clients?

You can buy mailing lists from list brokers, but they can be costly. You might try instead to obtain a list from the local humane society in exchange for a donation. Or better yet, make it a goal to participate in a few community events this year, where you can gather names and addresses in exchange for a valued gift such as a raffle prize. This type of participation gives you an opportunity to interact with potential new clients, see familiar faces and patients you already care for, and introduce your practice to a wider audience. To be effective, your list must be targeted, as general direct-mail programs are considered successful with a 2 percent return rate. Veterinary practices do not have the capital to create programs for which a 2 percent return is considered respectable; therefore, other avenues to reach prospective clients are preferred.

You might also want to consider partnering with related businesses. For instance, if there is a doggy day care or animal boarding facility in your area, introduce yourself to the owner of the establishment and determine whether that business might be willing to partner on some outreach efforts. Their clients are clearly willing to spend money on ancillary services for their pets, so they could be a good target audience.

⬛➡ **Do It Now**

Create a list of businesses in your area that might be good partners and who share a similar clientele. Devise a strategy to contact each one to determine how you might help each other grow your businesses.

What type of mailings and/or offers work best when we are doing a mass mailing?

The answer to this question depends on the goal for the mailing. Each marketing action should have a specific purpose and associated goal, which provides direction for the concept of the ad and makes it easier to measure results. The target audience should be clearly defined and segmented so that as many recipients as possible are true potential clients. Your message will likely take a different tone if you are mailing to current clients with whom you have an established relationship versus potential clients with whom you have yet to establish that trust and rapport. Likewise, every advertisement needs to have a call to action. People receiving your mailing need to know what to do with it and when, such as "Call now to take advantage of our spay and neuter special, good through August."

It is always advisable to use images or photos that have some relation to the copy so that you reinforce the message. As previously mentioned, however, avoid the temptation to provide too much information, and keep the ad focused on one product or service, or as few as possible if presenting them as a bundle.

All advertising materials should have a similar look, feel, and design reflecting your overall brand identity. Ultimately, you are looking to create instant recognition when someone sees your piece, just as people recognize a Target ad by the red bull's eye.

29

Besides our phone book listing and website, how do I communicate with people who are not current clients?

The telephone directory and websites are passive outreach efforts, meaning that prospective clients have to go looking for you. This is fine for one avenue, as you want to be reachable if sought.

To actively reach more potential clients, however, you must determine whom in your geographic region you want to reach. This is the concept behind targeting, also known as segmentation. As discussed in Chapter 1 on message and brand development, if you have segmented your audience and identified ideal clients for your practice, you can then select places to appear in person, putting you in direct contact with them. Or you may consider advertising in a publication that potential clients are likely to read, creating awareness of your practice and services.

Targeting a specific audience will always produce better results because it gives you an opportunity to speak directly to a smaller segment of people in terms that are relevant to them, and to address the specific needs or desires of a particular group. For instance, most horse owners also have dogs, and many have cats too. Consider investigating some equine publications or trade groups that may have a clientele similar to the ones you desire, and then determine the best way to get in front of this audience. This takes ingenuity and planning, but when you hit on an effective target, you know there is more to explore.

Your neighborhood could also be a good source of referrals. Consider asking neighboring shops and offices if they will allow you to place brochures or cards in a visible spot at their places of business. If you have a community bulletin board in your practice, offer to return the favor.

30

What if our demographics are predominantly low to moderate socioeconomically? How should we reach out to them?

Understanding your potential clientele is critically important when attempting to reach out to an economically challenged pet-owning population. There may be cultural norms to consider as well. If your audience is likely to want or need only basic services, focus on those as well as providing a strong foundation of education so you can keep their pets as safe and healthy as possible.

This may be an excellent community for offering low-cost spay and neuter programs. This service can serve as a loss leader; although you certainly should not price this service so low that you are losing money, consider how you can offer these services cost-effectively for lower margins and use the visit as an opportunity to start a relationship with the pet owner or family. Stress the importance of sterilization, parasite control, proper socialization of pets, regular examinations, and so forth. Maybe these services are available on select days for a special price to help you deliver care in a financially responsible way.

Discounts, while discouraged in some other situations, may be more effectively used in a low- to moderate-income community because the alternative may be not seeking care at all, and other clinics may simply be out of reach economically.

Quality care should still be delivered, but you may choose to invest in items that generate more profit and to reduce expenses where possible, for example stocking only certain medications or not offering many retail products because of inventory cost. There is a place for this type of service; you need to know your community and work to satisfy the true needs of the population, while still making a profit.

31

Is it effective to market to clients who have not been active for a few years, but were once good clients? If so, what strategies work best?

This is a bit tricky because you do not know whether the pet you cared for is now deceased. A good approach to marketing to clients who have not been in for a while is to make a personal call to each one who passes the year mark without a visit. Hopefully, you'll have an opportunity to have a team member make personal contact, thank the client for her previous patronage, and ask whether there is anything you can do to help keep her pets healthy. If she is open to the idea, you may offer to include her in your electronic newsletter to stay on top of what is happening at the clinic or news about medical advances.

If you are unable to reach clients by telephone, a personalized mailer indicating you have missed them and would like to see them again soon is always nice. Include any recent changes to the practice, such as new personnel, services, hours, or other timely information. Perhaps an incentive to schedule a visit within 30 days will encourage some to take you up on the offer. However, if you have not reached or heard from a client in more than a year, you can probably make the account inactive in your system. It is also possible that former clients will notice you out and about participating in community events or in local communication channels, so that if they ever do need veterinary services again, they will know where to turn and that they will be welcomed.

32

We all know that word of mouth is still the best marketing tool, but what is the second?

There are a few next-best marketing methods. One method is to clearly serve a specific and dedicated audience. This may be counterintuitive, as most practices try to serve as many pets and pet owners as possible and thus focus on a very broad audience and geographic radius. But it has been proven time and time again that if you can segment your audience—choosing a core population of pet owners that you would like to serve and then developing services to specifically meet their needs—you can become the clear and compelling choice or "go-to" practice. If you do a good job of satisfying a targeted audience, in short order those satisfied clients will tell others about you.

Another method is to simply become known throughout your community—create awareness by serving that community. As discussed in Chapter 6 on public relations, you will give back, contribute to good causes, gain awareness, and build your reputation at the same time. And you probably will have fun, too.

Beyond these more obvious solutions for marketing your practice, location matters, which, of course, speaks to how effective signage can be. If you are considering a move, visibility and great signage can work wonders for new business. Keep in mind that population shifts and consider locating in a newly developed area that is still growing.

Make friends with the local media. If you have a noteworthy story to tell that covers a range of human interests, put together a compelling pitch to the media and get some exposure for your practice.

Building a service business in many ways is also about numbers. The more visible you are, the more places you appear in service to the community, the greater the likelihood you will garner new clients. So get out there, and empower your team to be out there as well representing your practice.

33

What are the best ways to improve internal marketing?

Internal marketing, also known as inside sales, is most often thought of as reaching out to current clients of a practice and providing more services to this active list of pet owners who already consider you their animal's health care provider. So let's start here, and then let's offer a different perspective on internal marketing in the next question, also regarding internal marketing.

Most practices work hard to gain compliance on recommended services. But we all can do better, which is where internal marketing efforts are typically aimed. Because veterinary practices often service a wide variety of clientele, it is important to reach as many people as possible in the manner in which they prefer to be contacted. This requires that the practice be tuned in to its clients' needs. Ideally, you want to reach clients where they are and however it is most convenient for them, by offering the choice of text, email, telephone, or mail.

Frequency of contact is also important. To gain greater compliance and create stronger loyalty, it is important to reach your clients throughout the year, not just at annual vaccination time. Develop a variety of outreach efforts that incorporate many communication media and you will find that your visits will increase. Use direct mail with redeemable incentives if you have a special on a retail over-the-counter (OTC) item. Use an email format for personalized, useful, and timely information regarding safety, breeds, and recall news. Follow up after visits or procedures with personal telephone calls or to encourage scheduling of an elective service such as a dental cleaning. Finally, confirm appointments by texting—a convenient, personal, but nonintrusive method to say you're looking forward to seeing them without bothering them during the day.

In summary, you can show you really care about your clients and patients by taking the time to get to know them, their names, and their preferences, and then by delivering on those details that create positive experiences. Do so frequently and consistently; most of all, make sure every member of your team understands that building relationships takes everyone and that all team members play a key role.

34

How can our practice take our internal marketing efforts to the next level?

One of the most exciting aspects of marketing involves the team—working to unify everyone and create job satisfaction, which is also known as internal marketing. Most people think of marketing as an external activity. The truth is, though, that the most successful companies spend just as much if not more time focused on their greatest asset, their team, as they do on the practice. Launching an external initiative without ensuring your internal systems are designed to deliver is like burning money. What's worse, you likely will not get a second chance to correct service snafus because unless you live at the North Pole, pet owners have many choices when selecting a veterinarian. Also see Question 11 for more tips to improve internal marketing.

Hire carefully those individuals who you know have the capacity to create experiences for clients that will keep them coming back. Engaged team members may cost a bit more up front in salary, but they save tremendously in the long run. You'll experience lower turnover costs and require fewer expenditures on marketing because a well-honed team will generate more word-of-mouth referrals. Committed team members are also quite good at helping you train and integrate new staff or, conversely, help the underperformers choose to offer their services elsewhere.

Best of all, when you have team members who work in unison toward a common goal, they do so with great pride, and that translates out into the community. Your team members are your best billboards, not to mention that they make for a more enjoyable place to work. So spend some time and energy on your team, and your internal marketing efforts will get a whole lot easier!

35

What are some ideas that we can feature in our reception and exam rooms to market to our clients?

It is safe to say that few clients are aware of all the services you offer. Include printed materials that are professionally designed and written in language clients can understand with information on your most important services. Include your website address so clients can visit and access more information at a convenient time. If you have an electronic newsletter or some other form of communication that you send out by email, make sure copies are also included in your lobby and exam room materials. Encourage clients to opt in to these types of communication so you have an opportunity to provide them with other timely, important information regarding their pet's health. For instance, when taking a history, a technician could hand the client a brochure on dental health, suggesting it's time for Fluffy's cleaning.

In addition to educational information, clients always like to read about people who are similar to them. Keep albums with pet owner thank-you notes, photos, and testimonials to bridge the wait time, all the while showing how many people and pets you have helped, further bonding clients to you. You might even add a short case study near each testimonial with date, diagnosis, treatment, and outcome. These will undoubtedly trigger good questions, leaving a great opening for you to assuage any concerns of the pet owner that day.

In a prominent place in your lobby, place brochures from CareCredit or other third-party payment options. Not everyone is comfortable initiating a discussion of financial issues related to their pet's care, so making such information readily visible and available may help spark a necessary conversation.

How do we convince clients that certain vaccines, dental care, and other "discretionary" services are important?

If you believe that services such as vaccinations and dental care are in the pet's best interest, they are not discretionary. This is where you learn to develop all the communication skills you did not learn in vet school. Building rapport with clients gains trust and leads them to listen to and then go ahead with your recommendations. This skill can be learned, but it is one that takes practice. Making the recommendation, providing written literature, asking questions to learn the client's level of understanding, listening carefully between the lines for objections you need to overcome, and gaining compliance—these skills are both an art and a science, and are critical for your practice as well as your patients' health.

Many courses as well as books are available that will help you acquire the verbal skills you need, but nothing takes the place of practical application. It may seem a bit awkward at first, but if you sincerely believe that your patients will benefit by a certain level of care, then you are not selling anything other than your commitment to a healthy pet.

If you work in a multidoctor practice and observe that one or more veterinarians achieve greater acceptance of recommended services, ask whether you can listen in or participate in a few of their consultations so you can gain exposure to ways to present this type of information. We all have a sense of what feels natural, but we can always adapt ideas that others use to our own style to improve upon compliance.

37

How can I improve sales on food and retail products? How can I market them effectively to reluctant clients who would rather buy pet store, organic, or raw diets and think veterinary diets are simply a money grab?

As with any product or service you feel has significant value, there needs to be a clear and compelling reason for clients to consider buying what you stock. If you feel strongly about offering these particular products or services, you must educate clients and give them a reason to want to take your advice. If you've established rapport with your clients and consistently offered educational value during their visits, they probably already see you as an authority on their pets. Be sure to explain the research you have done in order to conclude that these are the best products in the category for your patients, and why. Also, specify how their pets will benefit and what they can expect by changing their diets.

To encourage clients to try a new nutritional product, consider offering a free second bag or a small discount on the first bag. You may even want to offer a money-back guarantee if their pet does not like the new food, which gives them assurance that it is perfectly safe and risk-free. You might also solicit feedback from clients who use these products to see whether they would be willing either to provide a testimonial or to be contacted by a client interested in their unbiased opinion of how the product affected their pet.

Most of all, your team needs to support your recommendations, so keep notes in the medical records and train your team to be accustomed to reading them so they can suggest an item at checkout time.

How do we convince clients that we are recommending the best and not just selling anything?

Communication could be part of the answer to almost every question in this book, but for this question in particular, it *is* the answer. Veterinary practices may provide a variety of services, from preventive and wellness care, vaccinations, and spay or neuter to more advanced surgical and diagnostic services. Some provide retail, nutrition, training, boarding, and grooming as well. Your practice needs to make a decision about which services to offer and to whom. As we know, not every pet owner is the target client for every practice, nor can every practice be right for every family. Whichever type of medical care and services you choose to provide, you must tailor your communication to your audience and what's best for them and their pets.

To make recommendations effectively, and thus gain compliance, a few things need to happen first. Some form of trust must be developed. This typically occurs over time, but what do you do with new clients? One way to establish trust is to ask good questions, and then be an excellent listener. Find out their concerns and direct your recommendations to satisfy those needs, while providing enough information to help them understand the most important thing you need them to know. Select language appropriate to the individual client, and to lend credibility you may want to cite studies, provide supporting literature, and even include "what can happen if I do" and "what can happen if I don't" scenarios to help them reach a decision that's right for them. If you are AAHA accredited, proudly display your certification and be sure to explain to all pet owners exactly what that means.

What can't be stressed enough is the importance of consistency. Once again, every member of your team needs to embrace the type of care you wish to deliver at your practice in order to gain the clients' trust, respect, and compliance for their pets' optimum health.

Ⅲ➡ **Do It Now**

Draft a document for your technicians, front-office staff, and veterinary staff containing the minimum standards of care you want each patient to receive on a regular basis. Include items such as dental cleaning, vaccinations, parasite control, senior blood screenings, and heartworm testing.

How do I increase client education without drowning my clients in information overload and on-hold messaging (which I personally loathe)?

Having a variety of educational tools at the ready to use in all circumstances will help you educate clients in the specific area that is relevant to them and their pets. Trying to teach pet owners about all aspects of their pets' health is not only unnecessary but also likely to cause more confusion than compliance.

The key to providing the right information at the right time is the art of good diagnosis. If you ask the right questions, you will elicit the knowledge you need to guide your client. A client with a new puppy or kitten may be given a new-pet packet that contains information on flea and parasite control, vaccination schedules, spay and neuter surgery, and what to do in an emergency. Conversely, a pet owner with a cat who is overweight may be given information on nutrition, weight management, and minimizing risk of diseases caused by this health problem.

Have a variety of pamphlets and information available in the waiting room and exam rooms for pet owners to pick up at their convenience. If you see they've chosen a particular pamphlet, engage them in a conversation regarding their reason for wanting to learn more about that topic. The more targeted and specific the information, the more likely clients are to understand and retain the message.

You can also include on your reminder cards, email newsletters, and invoices short tips about different topics with a call to action, such as "Visit our website for more information on the importance of spaying and neutering your pets."

▥➡ **Do It Now**

Select the top 10 reasons for a visit to the vet and be sure you have literature available for clients about how to know whether their pet should visit the vet.

40

How do we use marketing to increase our overall compliance?

Compliance is really all about education, so you need to think about the most effective way to give clients information about the best ways for them to keep their pets healthy. As discussed in Question 8 about branding, stick to one important topic and don't try to cram too much information into any message. See also Question 11 for more information on hiring and training your team to increase compliance.

The team needs to believe! Yes, it does take a team to increase compliance. As a group, decide which wellness services are most important and why. The entire staff needs to embrace this wellness philosophy if you are to be successful. Again, use a script to help each member of the team do his or her part to educate clients. For instance, when a client calls to schedule a pet's wellness exam, the receptionist may say something like "We look forward to seeing you and Tigger on Friday at 9:30 a.m. Be sure to ask Dr. Smith about a dental cleaning since it has been nearly two years, and our recommended intervals are normally 12 to 18 months." The client's electronic record can be flagged for "needing a dental." When the client and Tigger arrive, whoever greets them that day will see in their file that a dental cleaning should be recommended. Then, when the technician escorts them to the exam room to obtain a history, he or she can discuss the benefits of overall health by having regular dental cleanings. If the team has done a good job, by the time the doctor sees the patient and discusses the pre-anesthetic blood work to prepare for dental cleanings, the client will have already decided that Tigger needs this vital service and is already on board.

Another option, and one that works very well, is to create a compliance team of staff members who are particularly good at discussing these services. Have them make regular outreach calls to pet owners who have recently received a recommendation to make a particular appointment.

Knowing your current compliance rate will help you measure any increases you are able to create. Use your practice management software to gather data on compliance rates so you can set measurable goals for your team. You need a baseline in order to set realistic goals.

41

What are considered to be the "best practices" for wording and layout on appointment reminder cards or emails to maximize their effectiveness?

Anytime you communicate with a client, even if it is part of a larger mailing to a group of clients, it is important to write as if you were speaking to that client only. Personalization is vital for helping a client feel as though you care about him and his pet. Use his name and his pet's name in the correspondence. Any other unique indicators are helpful too, for instance a picture of the pet on the mailer. If not, use a picture of a pet of the same breed. Again, it makes the recipient feel as though you are speaking to him personally, which raises compliance.

As for layout, less is more. Make the correspondence easy to read, not cluttered with copy, and include a visual image that aligns with the copy message. Open with a headline. Next, augment the copy with a bold call-out or bullet points for emphasis. Then close with a call to action such as "Call now to schedule Buster's appointment at 555-1231," or "Now offering online appointment scheduling at appointments@abchospital.com. We look forward to seeing you and Buster soon."

42

How do I get clients whose pets are younger than 6 years of age to come in for "just a checkup"?

The key to compliance overall is building a relationship with your clients over time. So during the early years, it's important to educate them about services you recommend they do at least annually to give them the best opportunity to catch any health issues quickly. At each annual exam, let them know which types of screenings and examination you are doing, not just a general "he looks good." Explain what you are doing and the importance of the physical examination, what you check for, what the blood work reveals, the importance of the fecal, and so on. Because pets age much faster than we do, remind clients that as pets grow older, they should actually see the veterinarian more frequently because they are more susceptible to age-related conditions. Annual intervals are really much longer in pet years! If clients know the "why" behind the need for a physical and not just the "when" (annually), they exhibit greater acceptance.

The same is true for your staff. You can give them direction and expect them to carry it out, but if you tell them the reasons behind a procedure and how it helps contribute to the care of patients and the success of the practice, it is much more likely they will carry out your wishes, and cheerfully.

43

Are reminder cards sent from us as successful as those that are outsourced?

The key to reminder cards is consistency. Using an outside resource can make the process of sending out pet care reminders efficient. In today's modern veterinary practice, anything that can be automated, scheduled, or handled with the click of a button will, and typically does, increase compliance. Most of the good reminder services offer many marketing outreach products, cards being just one. Take advantage of the variety of resources available to help you decide what will work best for your practice.

Human participation will always be part of the equation, however. If you have the personnel resources to manage the additional time to gather the monthly list, print the cards, prepare them for mailing and/or emailing, and finally distribute them, there is nothing wrong with doing so in-house. Keep in mind that several people should be cross-trained to handle this important task, however it is done, so that you are not at the mercy of only one person who knows how to accomplish this task.

Whether you do so in-house or use an outside vendor, keeping a regular schedule and having appropriate follow-up to contact those who have not responded to the reminder will make the difference in your compliance statistics and the overall health of your patients.

Some reminder services will give you a free trial period. Consider taking advantage of this as an investment in increasing compliance. Based on the results, you will have your answer to this question.

44

How do I maintain my sense of professionalism while "marketing" my practice and not feel like a buffoon or a used-car salesman?

If you believe that pets need certain types of care to keep them healthy, and you know your practice can deliver these services in a professional and caring manner, why would you feel anything other than confident discussing them? Consider it your duty to inform your clients about best practices for their pets' health and wellness. If you are simply trying to increase the bottom line and are doing so disingenuously, you will feel uncomfortable.

One reason why people may be uncomfortable discussing their practice or service recommendations is that they have not thought about the responses they might give to clients' objections or questions. So prepare yourself. List all the doubts or resistance you may get about a recommendation and write responses to them that you can practice. When the time comes to discuss them, you'll feel more confident and not stumble over your words, making you appear unsure or as if you were pushing something their pets don't need.

It's important for you and your team to list the distinguishing characteristics of your practice so that you can describe it easily and clearly. For instance, "We are a small-animal veterinary practice that focuses on prevention and wellness care, including nutrition and weight management," or "We are an advanced care practice that provides general wellness diagnostics, including ultrasound for dogs and cats, and we have received accreditation from AAHA, the American Animal Hospital Association." What you need is an "elevator pitch," which is a concise, carefully planned, and well-practiced description of your company that your mother should be able to understand in the time it would take to ride an elevator.[1]

[1] The term "elevator pitch" is attributed to Robert Pagliarini of SeekingCapital.com.

ⅲ➡ **Do It Now**

Write an elevator pitch for your practice that everyone on the team can use when talking about or answering questions about your practice.

45

How do we track the productivity of charitable donations, community educational presentations, participation in trade shows with a booth, and so forth? Even if our client and patient numbers increase, can I attribute it to the PR or would it have happened anyway?

Public relations, or PR, is defined by the American Marketing Association as "That form of communication management that seeks to make use of publicity and other nonpaid forms of promotion and information to influence the feelings, opinions, or beliefs about the company and its products and services . . ." Given this definition, using PR is generally not designed to convert new customers directly. It is more a means to create awareness and manage a business's image in the public's view by use of third-party coverage.

As a practice, you will need to decide what you want to accomplish by taking part in activities outside your hospital. The more visibility you receive in front of pet owners whom you deem to be good candidates for clients, the better. So the question is, at what cost? If participation at an event has a fee attached and that fee is going to a charitable cause, then you know your participation will serve two important purposes and you can volunteer to participate if it fits your time and resource budget. If there is no charitable component, however, as with any other marketing decision you may make, doing your homework beforehand to determine the size of the audience relative to the cost will help you decide whether it is a worthwhile expenditure.

Measuring the results of this type of exposure is extremely difficult, but suffice it to say that it is the sum of your media mix that helps build a strong brand in the eyes of the community and serves to reinforce for your current clients that you are a good and honorable member of society.

Is it all right to use career fairs (for junior high and high school students) as an opportunity to advertise for our clinic?

This question can be interpreted in two ways. On the one hand, if the job fair is for high school students who might come work at your clinic and you wish to introduce the concept of careers in veterinary medicine, it may be an excellent venue and likely not too expensive. Most states have a shortage of skilled technicians, so this type of early exposure could spark interest in students who are not aware of work in the animal field.

On the other hand, if you are looking to gain new clients, a job fair at a high school is probably not a great resource. Remember, you need to speak directly to those who make the decision about who will care for the family pet and who will be paying for it. This is normally the pet owner or, in the case of a family, usually a parent. Children can influence these decisions, but there are better places to reach the people in charge of the family pet's health care than at a recruitment event at a high school.

47

How do I get the most from our local paper "Ask the Vet" articles I write?

Publishing a regular article in the paper is a great vehicle to generate name and face recognition in the community as well as to establish yourself as a trusted resource for all things pet related.

The style of writing should be informative but also exude compassion and honor the human-animal bond. This is a great opportunity to showcase your personality, that of the practice, and exactly what makes you different and special.

For maximum mileage from these articles, provide a link to the series on your website, including an archive section where people can read previously published answers. Encourage site visitors to write in with questions; you can be sure that any question submitted is one that many other pet owners have as well. If you own the rights to these articles, you might print them and compile a booklet to keep out in the practice lobby or exam rooms for pet owners to read while waiting.

If the paper publishes a feature article on you and your practice, have it professionally mounted and framed and hang it conspicuously in your practice for all to see!

How do I go about holding an open house?

The most important aspect of holding an open house is getting people to attend. There is nothing worse than throwing a party and having no one show up. Just as in every other undertaking, start with a plan. What do you hope to accomplish with the open house— essentially, what is the purpose and whom do you want to attend? Are you looking to thank your current clients, attract new clients, or both? After you have identified the why and the who, focus on the how: how to get people there, how to involve your team, how to garner support from your best vendors, and how to throw a fun, informative, and worthwhile event.

Don't skimp on invitations, party favors, signage, printed handouts, and food and beverages. If you are AAHA accredited, use this as an opportunity to provide information about the significance of this designation. Take advantage of the materials AAHA makes available to its accredited hospital members for open houses. Many of your vendors will be glad to help out with ideas, giveaways, raffle prizes, and the like. Your staff will also be a great source of creative resources and potentially guests. Make this a team effort, plan well in advance and publicize it, and you are sure to have a successful event.

Question 85 addresses the return on investment from an open house.

Ⅲ➡ **Do It Now**

Sit down with your team and create a list of all tasks and vendors you need to coordinate for a productive open house. Don't underestimate the amount of work and time it takes to throw a successful event. Plan accordingly.

49

How do I get our practice name out there into the community without excessive costs?

"Excessive costs" is a relative term. There will always be costs associated with operating your business profitably and sustaining a long-term legacy. If you are a new or early-stage practice, you will need to invest more to gain clients and build momentum to generate referrals. If you are more established, you will still need to actively and regularly communicate with current and prospective clients to let them know you care about them. It is all too easy for pet owners to respond to an attractive message or two from a competitor, especially if someone has also recommended another veterinary clinic in the area. Keep in mind that you are trying to build loyalty among your clientele, as those loyal to you are least likely to sample the competition and most likely to refer others.

The best marketing involves a variety of methods, similar to the concept of diversifying your investment portfolio. Not all avenues are directly measurable, but branding activities, direct mail (print and/or electronic), public relations, participation in charity events, advertisements, and a professionally designed website that is updated frequently are all important aspects of putting your best foot forward. Carefully choosing the best team possible to engage clients and deliver your services will help solidify your reputation for sustainable growth.

50

What are some "out-of the-box," unconventional ideas on how to creatively market yourself in your community?

The options are endless for making a splash in the community. The answer to this question lies in what is interesting to you and your team. Consider creating a charitable event that assists animals in need. Better yet, partner with a group that is already doing so, one you trust that has the reputation with which you would like to be associated. Together you could create twice the fanfare. Of course, pitch the story to the media or ask a local PR firm to help you get coverage for the event.

Think about other businesses that might enjoy an alliance with your practice. For instance, contact your local Red Cross and have a blood drive for pets and people. Or contact the local gym to conduct a seminar on physical fitness for people and their pets.

As an example, one cardiology group sponsors a wonderful event every year for a children's hospital cardiac wing. It is a reunion for all current and former cardiac patients. The kids love to see the dogs and cats that are also cardiac patients, and the hospital is grateful for the support. It is an event that everyone looks forward to each year, and it has become a highlight of the community.

There is no shortcut for creating awareness in your community. You must be part of your community to become well-known. Take advantage of the hobbies you enjoy to create synergy among multiple groups to bring together many more than you might on your own.

ⅠⅢ➡ Do It Now

Start a scrapbook of ideas from PR and marketing pieces of other businesses. This might include ads, events, and website features. These will help you come up with your own unique solutions.

51

What factors influence a potential client to choose our facility over another based on the Web or print ad? What language and phrases catch clients' attention?

One of the reasons advertising, as a form of marketing, needs to be conducted continuously is that it is often a matter of timing. Remember, one aim of advertising is to satisfy a perceived need better than some other resource. Thus, a well-written and well-designed ad may capture the attention of someone in the market for veterinary services.

If you have decided that advertising on a community website or in a newspaper will reach your intended audience, then create multiple ads and rotate them. This will keep the ad focused on one key message. Also, because different people will respond to different messages, if you advertise your key advantages over the course of three or four ads, you are more likely to capture the largest group of potential clients with a message that is relevant to them. You have the opportunity to build interest over time. Perhaps a reader sees your ad one week, and the next week they see another one of your ads showcasing a different service. This tells them you are versatile and multifaceted in your offerings. You must also keep the ad fresh so that viewers will notice rather than ignore it.

Be creative and resist the temptation to create an ad that looks or sounds like other veterinary ads. Ads, like the other materials you create, should reflect the personality of the practice and be distinguishable from others.

52

Should we advertise to all pet owners or target our own clients?

It's important to determine what your goals are before you embark on any outreach effort. You must be in touch with your current clients on a fairly regular basis for a number of reasons, such as reminding them of vaccinations and other services, or informing them of new services, changes in personnel, or hours of availability. An even better reason is to let them know you care about them, which can be done by providing them with regular, consistent, and valuable information that benefits their pets.

However, if there is a specific service you want to promote, it makes sense to target the segment of your clientele who would benefit most from that service, in order to avoid overloading other clients with information for which they have no need. You would not want to direct a cat-related service at dog owners, for instance. Targeting has many benefits. You maximize your costs by directing the outreach only to an audience of people who are most likely to take advantage of the service or information. You can also be specific in the copy and provide details for this group of pet owners. This will increase the percentage of clients who respond favorably. Both types of marketing are important, but segmenting your audience for certain products or services makes a lot of sense (and cents).

As for advertising to all pet owners, a percentage of your marketing dollars should be invested in generating new clients. We discuss this at length in Chapter 4 on acquiring new clients.

53

If we place an ad, what size is best for a small-animal practice?

Advertising is just one of many marketing tools available to you. It is not possible to make a general recommendation regarding size. Think about what you are trying to accomplish with the ad and where it will appear. You may have many choices besides size, such as color, placement location, and frequency of run, that dictate the cost.

Before you place a print or electronic ad, get the publication's media kit with all the demographics so you can verify the expected readership and make sure it is an investment worth making. In general, ads are best run over time, as few onetime runs will generate much business. It may take multiple appearances of an ad before it even registers with a reader, and that assumes the ad is well produced. You may want to try a three-month run in a publication that coincides with a particular issue or timely event. Then, of course, be sure to track all sources of new clients to determine whether any of them saw the ad.

We often are asked to advertise in a local school's theater program. Will this actually help to bring in clients, as these advertisements are often a lot of money?

Placing one ad in one publication one time is unlikely to generate much new business for any type of establishment. The kind of advertisement you are inquiring about seems geared more to support the theater program at the school. If that is an area of interest for you, you might consider such a media buy. But if your goal is to generate new clients, this typically is not a good investment.

If you enjoy supporting the local school and extended educational community, consider supporting a school athletic team, where your signage and recognition for your practice can be showcased at every game and in the season program. You may even get a logo imprinted on the uniforms if you are a large enough sponsor. Not only will you become a valued member of the school community, but every opponent's cheering squad will be exposed to your name and logo. And if that team wins, your visibility can grow beyond the neighborhood—so root, root, root for the home team!

Another way to support the community in a way that provides a broader reach than a onetime ad in a program or similar publication is participation in a holiday food/supplies drive that benefits people and pets. Consider making your facility a drop-off location, and ask your clients to spread the word for you by forwarding email announcements and flyers on your behalf. You could even tie such a drive into a program to generate new clients by offering a free pet exam for those who donate a specified amount of goods. You may not need to offer the incentive to get donations, but you are likely to generate new business and goodwill along the way.

Are print ads or billboards of any value in our profession?

Any ad with the right message in the right place in front of the right people has the potential to be successful. It very much depends on your market. Advertisements and billboard ad prices vary wildly across the country and different demographics. For example, a veterinarian in South Dakota has had great success booking a billboard during pheasant-hunting season on the main road heading back into town. It is clearly visible to hunters, and each year she gains several new patients as a result. The cost is reasonable, which helps make this a viable option. But she has taken the concept one step further. At a nearby hotel where hunters stay during the season, she has introduced herself as a local resource for hunting dogs as well as other personal pets. The hotel has enjoyed this resource and helped hunters who inquire about veterinary care in the area by referring them to her. As a bonus, because she has made so many hotel guests happy, a few of the hotel employees have also become clients.

There can be many goals in placing an advertisement. You may simply want to support a publication, such as a veterinary medical association newsletter or a local community homeowners' association flyer. More often than not, these ads create awareness, but they also can generate business if you offer a service needed by the readers. If the ad is well done, it might just be the catalyst to motivate someone to give your practice a try.

Is a short-term discount program (such as dental health month) a real benefit to the practice, or are we just attracting people who would have had it done anyway and making less money on the deal in the process?

An easy way to determine the value of a short-term discount program is to run a report from your electronic medical records system to see how many sevices were performed as a result of the program. For example, if you publicized and promoted a discount for dental month, how many dentals did you ultimately do? The results are contingent on gathering accurate information, so your staff should be accustomed to tracking results of promotions. Otherwise you will have no hard facts to help you determine whether you should run the discount again or modify it in some way. You can then take this year's data and compare them against previous years when similar promotions were run. Keep in mind that there are other variables that will affect whether pet owners choose to have a dental done on their pets and when, so the results should be understood as more of an indication than hard facts.

Promotions for a specific service such as dental month should be considered an awareness push *and* an effort to get as many clients in as possible for the service and education. If you have never tracked this information before, try having a few of your team members focus on compliance that month by following up on all reminder cards with a telephone call to schedule a visit for the dental special. If a call results in a scheduled appointment, you can consider this appointment one that would have been unlikely to happen without the additional effort to encourage a best practices wellness service.

If you are not inclined to offer a discount (see Question 22), consider offering a bundled package of services so that you are not discounting the dental per se, but providing the pre-op blood work, dental cleaning, antibiotics, and nail trim for a set price, for instance. Many people will respond to a value proposition like this and feel as though they are getting a good deal by receiving additional services beyond the normal dental care. If you are trying to promote a particular service, by all means track the results and then measure the number of visits less program administration costs to see how you fared.

57

How do we decide which marketing promos (e.g., senior discounts, monthly percent-off specials) are worthwhile and which should be scrapped?

To make business decisions based on real information as opposed to shooting from the hip requires that you make time to review the results of marketing initiatives as a standard best practice. Therefore, what *can* be measured *should* be measured. To use your marketing dollars most cost-effectively, determine measurable metrics beforehand, so that you can track the outcome, or at least portions of it. To do this well, all of your staff need to know about each promotion or marketing message. This may sound obvious, but often just a few members of the team are involved in creating and executing a marketing tactic, so the intent and delivery are communicated to the team only in a cursory manner or not at all. With staff working different shifts, your internal communication channels often make the difference between engaging staff and not. Staff must be able to encourage adoption of promotions when speaking with clients, and understand why they are asking clients questions regarding awareness of these promotions or whether the promotion is what motivated the client to come in for a visit. Staff awareness is important for any of the clinic's marketing messages.

Another consideration when deciding which promotions are worthwhile concerns your health care philosophy and those services you feel are vitally important for pets. For these services, you and the team will want to do everything possible to encourage clients to take advantage of the savings and get the recommended care for their pets. If your practice sees a lot of overweight pets or diabetic cats, for instance, you may want to focus attention on services related to nutrition or senior feline screenings. Evaluate your patients and how they present. You and the team can then determine which services will benefit your patients most. Then educate your clients about excellent health care for their pets.

How do I most effectively promote our new puppy and kitten wellness packages?

The best way to promote a particular service is to reach those that need it. Consider creating relationships with local area shelters that adopt out puppies and kittens, and get a spot on their lists of local veterinarians who offer a free first exam to all newly adopted animals. Think about where else you might reach puppy and kitten owners, such as breeders. Research the local breeder and breed rescue groups in your area and offer to speak at their next meeting about pet care and any breed-specific conditions for which they should be on the lookout. You can introduce the puppy and kitten package there, obtain email addresses, and continue to reach out to this attentive group. Another avenue might be aligning with dog trainers who offer puppy kindergarten classes, local day care, or pet resorts. The more people who know you have this service, the more likely you are to receive referrals and find pet owners who want to take advantage of it.

Make sure you have good materials to give to these referring sources that explain the highlights and key benefits of the program. In addition, include information about the service on your website along with testimonials from people who used the package about the value it has brought them and their pets. Having other people tell their stories to your prospective clients always lends another layer of credibility, and you are sure to receive more volume because of it.

Finally, be absolutely certain that your staff members are well trained in discussing this important service. After all, if clients have good experiences when their pets are puppies or kittens, and you have established your practice as the best place to care for their pets, you have the opportunity to build long-term relationships and turn them into loyal clients who provide revenue over the life of their pets and serve as referral sources.

Do specials such as one for dentistry during dental month have a positive impact on the practice (other than the practice's income)?

Besides greater income, there are many other reasons why you will experience a positive effect from such specials. First, more pets seen at the clinic means that more are receiving the recommended care. There will also be cases in which you notice other issues during the examination that might not have been caught otherwise. So from a preventive standpoint, an extra examination a year is a good thing. If you routinely perform a pre-op blood screen before anesthesia, this is another chance to catch a problem before it becomes untreatable.

Most important, however, is an additional opportunity to further bond with pet owners and provide more education about keeping their pets in optimum health. This "face time," if handled well, will drive new revenue in the future. Consider a short intake questionnaire for every pet owner to fill out upon check-in that asks a few simple questions about their knowledge of a particular condition their pet may be susceptible to at its current age. Use the answers to stimulate discussion and a question-and-answer session during the examination. Good questions are part of the art of good conversation, and you can learn a lot about what pet owners need to know by assessing their current knowledge base and using your expertise to fill in the gaps.

Trust takes time to develop, and every opportunity you get to nurture that relationship and support the human-animal bond brings you one step closer to a client for life.

What should I do if I receive a bad online review?

Exchanging information online is extremely easy today, making for great advantages in promoting your practice, but it can also pose risks that need to be managed. Let's hope that you are made aware of any scenario in which a client is angry or dissatisfied in any way, so you can take the opportunity to remedy it as quickly as possible. Learning about it for the first time by reading a negative posting online means you probably have gaps in service or, at a minimum, in communication with your clients. It is not possible to please everyone, but it typically takes a good deal of motivation to share an opinion online—good or bad.

If you receive a review that is less than stellar and you know who the author is, make every effort to correct the situation. The best way to avoid this problem is not only to be on top of your game all the time and have clients leave your practice thrilled, but also to encourage those who are longtime or raving fans to post their experiences online. Over time, the glowing reviews will far outshine any negative comments, and most savvy consumers will acquiesce to the trend rather than the errant remark.

61

How do we use Facebook and our website in marketing clients?

Using social media is all about building community. A communication tool such as Facebook allows you to broaden your reach and directly access a far larger audience than you could by traditional methods, and more cost-effectively. The beauty of Facebook is the way it's designed: Every time someone "likes" your page, it is announced to all of his or her friends and your exposure multiplies.

It is important to understand that using social media is not free, unless you think of your staff's time as free, which of course it is not. You should have a specific plan and purpose for keeping a Facebook page, just as when employing any other communication tool. If you have the resources, personnel, and time to effectively reach out and engage pet owners who would enjoy being a part of your community, Facebook can be an outstanding avenue to amass an audience.

Be sure your Facebook link is prominently displayed on your website to encourage visitors to check out your page and become fans. Additionally, make sure all of your practice's information is accurate and easily available on your Facebook page, along with an array of photos representative of your clinic. Because Facebook and the Web are both electronic tools, you gain the benefit of people finding your website on Facebook and vice versa. In essence, the tools support each other well and allow you to "point" visitors where you want them to go for information you recommend.

How can I make the most of technology (e.g., Internet advertising, Facebook, blogs, online coupons)?

Making the most of technology could take up a whole chapter, or book for that matter. However, in short, you want to integrate as many tools as possible with the goal of making it easy for people to find you, access your clinic, and accomplish what they need to in a streamlined fashion. Take down the barriers to more business. For instance, after you have built and launched your website, make sure all other online tools, such as Facebook, banner ads, and columns you write for other publications, link to your website.

Technology allows clients to communicate with you in convenient ways. Consider using online appointment scheduling, texting clients to confirm appointments, and emailing patient files and diagnostic images. No one likes to be on hold for a long time or to play telephone tag. If clients can communicate via email or text with their veterinary clinic, it will save time (and therefore money), and you will be viewed as progressive, accommodating, and client-focused.

One way to gauge the types of technology that are most client-friendly is to ask your youngest generation of staff what would be desirable if they were clients. You may just learn a whole new language. For each new suggested use of technology, you will also need to consider whether it will be useful to your clients and when it would be appropriate to adapt it. Not every new technology is right for your practice. It always depends on your clientele.

What is the best way to drive clients to our website?

Before you guide traffic to your website, make sure you have a site you are proud of and one that is easy to navigate. The type should be large enough for people to read comfortably, and it should have a clean design without too much clutter, include good photography, and be updated on a regular basis to keep it fresh and current.

Getting people to your site can happen in many ways. The most obvious is to provide your URL, or website address, on all printed materials. This includes business cards, brochures, trade show banners, direct-mail pieces, newsletters, promotional items, fax cover sheets, and letterhead stationery.

Anytime you communicate electronically, be sure to embed a link to your website into the document. For instance, create a signature file at the bottom of your email so that all of your contact information, including your website address, is automatically attached to each new email. This also means that your email address should consist of yourname@yourpracticewebsite.com. If you have a website, there is no reason to use a yahoo, hotmail, or gmail account. Don't miss this important branding opportunity by marketing one of the major Internet players—they get enough publicity. Instead, market your own practice! Additionally, when you send anything via email, include hyperlinks to your site for more information. When posting on Facebook or Twitter, do likewise and you will create a pipeline of visitors from many places.

Finally, create relationships with other websites to provide a link to your site. For one thing, it could introduce another audience to you. Even better, the more sites that link to your website, the higher your search engine ranking.

⇒ **Do It Now**

If you do not have an email address with your practice domain name, create one. Call your IT support for assistance. Vow to market your own business!

How can I better market my online store?

If you want to increase your retail sales, it is wise, once again, to use the entire team to bolster revenue. You may find it helpful to set goals, in measurable amounts over a specific time period, in order to track progress. Then discuss the goals with your staff and get them on board as to why you want to increase retail sales, what that increase will mean to the practice, and how they can help. Once you have an understanding of common goals, you are ready to begin marketing the store.

The most obvious method to increase visitors is to prominently place a link to your store on the home page of your website. But simply placing the link there will not be enough. You must also communicate the benefits of buying from you and let visitors know what they will find once inside. Then group complementary products together so that you can capture the largest transaction with each shopping experience.

Make sure you let clients know you have an online store where they can conveniently shop and get all the products you sell at the practice and more. Include information about your store on any client materials, such as reminder cards, electronic communications (include a hyperlink), advertisements, and brochures. In short, if you want to move goods, you need to get people to your store by first letting them know it exists and what benefits they will experience from buying through you.

For everything you sell in the practice, you might consider placing stickers on the goods that say something like "To reorder this product online, go to www.yourpractice.com/onlinestore." Make it easy to read and visible.

Whom should I put in charge of our website and social networking accounts to maintain consistent messaging: someone in the clinic or an outside entity?

Having the responsibility to "speak" for the clinic is a big one, so choosing the right person to handle your social media is critically important. If you wish to participate in this process as the owner of the practice, by all means do so. Otherwise, a manager you trust to speak on the clinic's behalf is probably the best person to assign this task. Keeping it in-house helps you control the messaging, helps maintain the timeliness of the communication, and gives you a better opportunity to view comments posted each day.

If you do not have someone you trust to manage these accounts on a regular basis, or if your team simply does not have the time, it may be wise to outsource. The key to outsourcing successfully is having a plan and clear expectations for the type of information you want to be shared on your behalf as well as how frequently and, even more important, what you do *not* want posted. Even if you do outsource, you should check your page frequently to get a true picture of what your practice is putting out there and how the information is being received.

How do we create emails that clients will actually open?

Just like any good advertisement, an email needs to be well written and compelling. The key to email success is the subject line. Think of it as a headline to grab attention and somehow convey enough importance to be opened. But keep it honest—no bait and switch or you may anger the reader.

If your clients have given you their email addresses for electronic communications, chances are most will be opened, but you can increase this likelihood by being cognizant of your clients' time and making sure that anytime you communicate with them you are providing information that will be deemed valuable (educational), enjoyable (fun), or timely (product recall).

Think about the timing and frequency of your communications also. It is important to be in touch with clients on a regular basis, but getting the frequency right is also part of being there to provide helpful information without being annoying. The content of your emails will also help to determine how often they should be sent. Give some thought to when during the week would be a good time for clients to receive communications. Monday mornings, for obvious reasons, would not be the best choice. Create a schedule, but be cognizant of holidays, conflicts with other important communications, and the like, so yours can be a welcome item in the in-box.

Additionally, make clients feel safe by clearly stating your privacy policy at the bottom of the emails and allowing them to opt out at any time. This will make their participation and engagement feel voluntary, which should enhance the relationship.

67

How do we get more email addresses from clients to promote communication and marketing via email?

If you would like to communicate with clients via email, as they come in as new clients or for scheduled appointments, make this request part of your client forms, even for drop-off appointments. To help clients feel comfortable providing their email addresses, be sure to include a privacy policy so they understand how their email will be used.

It is advisable to use an online email communication tool such as Constant Contact® or iContact so that you can assure clients of the ability to opt in, opt out, and pass along emails to others. This gives your clients peace of mind that if they wish to stop receiving mail, they can do so independently.

You should also have a sign-up link on your website, preferably the home page, and a contact page where people can sign up to receive email from you as a means to stay in touch. Don't forget to include this sign-up information on other materials, such as your invoices, reminder cards, printed newsletters, advertisements, and brochures. If your practice is in the habit of calling to confirm appointments, you might ask clients during those calls whether you could obtain their email address to confirm future appointments. Point out that they can easily reach the office electronically if they need to change the appointment. In this manner, you offer your clients two-way communication, which is really what we all want—to know we are heard as well as a means to get information when needed.

Do It Now

If you do not yet have a written privacy policy to share with clients, write one and place it on all materials that ask them for personal information.

How do I determine the value of money spent on interactive websites with client-specific profiles? Many clients love this service but many others have never signed up.

Pet owners love personalization, and interactive websites offer a great way to help clients feel personally connected to their pets' information and their veterinarian. Even though there may not be an easy way to determine that actual value in monetary terms, anytime you can further bind clients to you and your practice by having them actively engage in online features for their pet, you reap rewards in loyalty, which often translates into more visits and more referrals.

Simply having a tool, though, is not enough. The availability and benefits of the tool need to be promoted to help clients find value in using it. Otherwise, the tool offers no value to the practice. Clients who have not yet taken advantage of this service may need to be reminded about the benefits and even offered assistance in getting started. This is an area your front-office team should be able to chat about knowledgably so they can help clients establish an account. Consider creating a short "how-to" handout or step-by-step instructions for activating and using this free service. Make it benefit oriented and include instructions for accessing more information or help if needed. If you want to get clients on board, provide instructions that will make the process easy.

Assuming that clients need to hear a message several times to make it effective, how much email marketing does it take to become offensive to the average client?

A lot more than you think. An old marketing adage is "A prospect needs to see or hear your marketing message at least seven times before taking action and buying from you." There are many reasons for this. There is a lot of clamor out there for your clients' attention, and it's hard to cut through this noise. This is why your emails should be well designed and well written, and should deliver something of value to the recipient. Every message, whether in print or electronic, should have a headline and then more detailed information on the core message, and close with a call to action. Provide a link, phone number, or information on taking the next step front and center.

Marketing may also be a matter of timing; people may not need you—yet. Or maybe they don't feel they know or trust you well enough to act on your recommendation. By providing free information to your clients and prospects on a regular basis, though, you are building a solid relationship. Information offered in a newsletter or blog doesn't set off alarms because it's not a sales pitch; it's a genuine attempt to educate and help.

Also remember that it never hurts to ask. If you periodically survey your clients about their communication preferences, be sure to ask, on a scale of 1 to 5, how they feel about the frequency of emails, and leave room for them to share what they like about the emails, or suggest other things they would like to hear about.

70

What is the best way to reach the 25–35 age group with information about our practice?

The first question you should ask yourself is, why are you looking to reach this age group specifically? Do the demographics of your area skew young and therefore you want to capture a larger percentage of younger clientele? If that's the case, then chances are you have a fair number of 25- to 35-year-olds working in your practice. Ask them what type of marketing they respond to and how would they like to be communicated with regarding their pet's health care.

It is likely that the generation who grew up with access to a computer, cell phone, copy machine, and video games has technology wired into their genes. They probably don't read a conventional newspaper but instead get their news from modern television satire shows, the Internet, or a favorite blog.

Not only are the sources of information now different than for previous generations, but it is delivered differently. With short attention spans and an eye for the visual, this age group requires that you provide quick and easy connections to the services they need. Otherwise, it is just as easy for them to skip over to the next option. So make scheduling appointments online easy and hassle-free. Allow people to access their pets' medical records through a portal and keep your website up-to-date, uncluttered, and full of bold headlines for simple and straightforward navigation. Confirming appointments by text will be appreciated, and receiving any follow-up instructions electronically will be considered a given.

If you are still printing on paper and faxing information, it's time to embrace a new world of communication or you will get left behind, and quickly.

71

How effective are email reminders versus mailed reminders?

Whether email or printed reminders are more effective depends on several factors. The best part about email reminders is that you can track their "open" rate to see how many get read—something you cannot do with postal mail. If your website is set up to allow for online appointments, the reminder can link clients to scheduling an appointment right then and there, making it that much more effective. If you make it simple, your conversion rate will increase. You should be investing in this type of technology.

Both email and mailed reminder results can be tracked. Every time someone schedules an appointment, your practice management software should show that the user received a reminder and the service requested. Regular monthly reports should clearly outline the activity generated as a result of your reminder outreach efforts. If you are not getting these reports or need assistance in understanding them, consult your reminder service provider help you to learn to interpret the data so you can gauge their effectiveness and watch for trends over time.

Ultimately, how you reach out to your clients should be determined by who your clients are and what they prefer. In due time, electronic options for communicating with veterinarians will become the norm, so the sooner you get comfortable adapting new technologies to the desires of your clientele, the better for all—and most of all, for pets!

72

Is it worth spending tens of thousands of dollars on a website developer to create and maintain our hospital's website? If yes, why? If no, why not?

The short answer is no, it should not cost tens of thousands of dollars to create and maintain a professional website. It is important, however, that you engage a professional Web development firm to build your practice website, as this is probably the most important and visible tool you have for speaking to your clients, prospective and current. Just its design will tell visitors a lot about you, so it is critical to be deliberate in what you say and how you use images and information. Professional services are not inexpensive, but do not select your website vendor based on price alone. There are many other considerations:

Website Do's

- Engage a Web development firm that understands the animal health care industry.
- If you have the time to devote to keeping your site current, have a content management system built for your site so you can do a lot of the work yourself.
- If you do not have the time to devote to keeping your site current, have a regular plan to provide information to the website maintenance company so they can update the site for you.
- Frequently introduce new information and keep information accurate and timely.
- Use common and simple search engine optimization functionality, such as having others link to you, to help your site appear as high up in the listing as possible.
- Hire a professional photographer to take pictures of your facility and your team at work for the website.

- Use a professional copywriter to prepare copy specifically for the Web.
- Do use an email address @thenameofyourpractice.com.

Website Don'ts

- Do not believe you can write copy and design the site yourself and have it adequately represent who you are, unless you are a designer and developer.
- Do not believe anyone who tells you they can guarantee you placement in search engines.
- Do not launch your site and avoid touching it again for years. It is a living, breathing part of your practice.
- If you have a website, do not use an email address @anyname otherthanyourpractice.com.

73

How do I determine the best website search engine or listing to use (e.g., Google, Yahoo, LocalVets?)

Simply by having a website, you have a presence on the Web and in search engines. That does not mean, however, that you will be satisfied with your ranking. Many things can enhance your placement in the search engine rankings, such as updating your site frequently, putting a title with a commonly searched phrase on each page, and using key words and phrases in the copy on each page. Be careful with this last suggestion, though, because search engines calculate ratios—if you use too many key words and phrases, the engines read that as abuse, and if you use too few, you may not get the recognition you seek. Work with a skilled developer to maximize your ranking simply by building your site well. It need not be a situation that requires a monthly investment.

Links to your site on other sites are also a great tool to build your ranking, so partner with others to provide a direct link to your website.

Another area to investigate is your local phone company or telephone book. If you have a presence in the phone book, it may come with an online listing that is free or costs a small monthly fee. Be sure the placement on the search engine page is desirable to you before you commit to this fee, though, even if it is small. The local telephone company may offer a similar service for an online presence, so be sure to ask about the options.

If you would like to investigate additional online marketing avenues, be sure you are comparing apples with apples when presented with the programs these sites offer. Most important is having your ad targeted to those most likely to need and use your service.

74

How can I determine our marketing budget for the year, and what percentage of gross revenue should I spend on advertising?

The amount to spend on marketing should be directly related to what you want to accomplish; then work backward to determine what that will cost. A key determinant is also the stage the business is in. If you are a fairly new business, you'll likely need to spend more money than if you are a more mature one. But again, it depends on your situation—your demographics; competition, if any; the visibility of your practice; its reputation; and so on. The most important aspect of marketing is that any outreach effort be part of a larger overall plan and not be conducted ad hoc or on a whim when things get slow. You will gain the most traction and spend less money overall if your messaging is consistent, concise, and creative.

New businesses or ones that are in a position of rebranding may pay up to 10 percent of revenue to accomplish goals in line with these initiatives. More mature practices may invest 3 to 7 percent of annual revenue to maintain a fresh, interactive, and broad-based marketing program. Anything less than this is reserved for businesses that have little competition, those that have developed a very effective method of consistent communication and feedback with their clientele, and those that receive the majority of their new clients by referral. If you are in this last group, it is still important to review your marketing plan regularly and not get complacent about what has worked in the past. That typically is not what will work in the future, so your ability to adapt is key to staying in a good position in the marketplace.

75

How much should I be spending on yellow pages advertising?

Every practice should track how new clients hear about it; this information should be gathered when processing a new client file. It then is easy to run regular reports to see which outreach efforts are driving new clients to the practice. If a sizable portion of new clients are coming in as a result of the yellow pages, then an argument can be made to continue with a presence in that publication. With new technology and other preferred means of sourcing a health care provider for a pet, though, it is more likely that few to no new clients actually schedule appointments as a result of an advertisement in the yellow pages. If that is the case, then you may want to consider only a basic listing there in one or more sections, depending on how the publication classifies its sections under "Veterinary Services." This often comes with an online listing as well, which is ideal.

It is important to know your practice's demographics and which types of sourcing information your audience uses to find a new resource for a desired product or service. As a general rule, whatever percentage of new business comes to you from the yellow pages should be the percentage of your advertising budget directed to this medium. For instance, if 10 percent of your new clients come to you as a result of seeing an ad in the yellow pages, then 10 percent of the funds you budget for marketing should go toward your yellow pages presence. The only practices that should give the yellow pages a bit more thought are those that have an emergency services component. But again, the percentage of clients coming to you as a result of the yellow pages ad should dictate how much you continue to spend there. In most cases, you can divert the funds once used for the yellow pages to refresh your website or pursue a newer, more popular method of reaching new clients.

⇒ **Do It Now**

Make a list of all your marketing efforts in a spreadsheet. Create a column
for the cost of each initiative, the time frame, and the corresponding result.
Then run the appropriate report to fill in the numbers to track trends. Adjust
accordingly.

76

How do I get the owners of the practice to support marketing and advertising efforts?

Many doctors think in very linear terms, just as they have been taught to examine, diagnose, and treat. Building and sustaining a profitable business are not so black and white. You might give them literature or case studies of how well-planned and well-executed marketing efforts greatly helped some businesses and what kinds of results they could expect. Maybe you can get a small budget allocated for testing out marketing and advertising; the results may lay the foundation for more support.

Moreover, practice valuation specialists and certified public accountants will tell you that up to 75 percent of a practice's value can be based on goodwill—the intangibles such as reputation, image, location in the community, and so on. Marketing, as you now know, is not simply an advertisement in a newspaper; it is everything you do, say, or make visible. Therefore, your facility, signage, uniforms, lobby décor, and website are all marketing—they all say something loud and clear about the practice. Ask the owners whether this is what they want to be saying. If not, you have a foot in the door to advocate for their support.

If the owners are happy with the current practice revenue and rate of new clients, then you will have a tough time convincing them they need to do anything different. But in today's climate, it's a rare practice that wouldn't want to increase its base of clients and revenues to support the delivery of optimum health care.

77

Which is considered the best use of marketing dollars: developing our website, creating brochures, or sending out a newsletter (by email or mail)?

The answer is all of the above. Each tool satisfies a different need and sometimes even different clients. Marketing is really a compilation of everything you do to communicate with current and prospective clients. Some tools are considered passive, such as a website where the client seeks you out, for instance when typing in your address or finding you in a search. A direct-mail piece, by contrast, is active, whereby you are making a concerted effort to reach a specific audience by mail, print, or electronic means. Brochures and other types of materials are tools to support the education process whereby you want to encourage specific behaviors to gain compliance in health care recommendations. The most effective marketing typically involves a variety of tools and tactics—what is often referred to as the "marketing mix."

Think about your clients as fitting into three categories: attract, retain, expand. Then ask yourself, what tools do I need to develop to attract new clientele? What tools do I need to employ to retain clients? And finally, how can I expand my relationship with clients and get more from them? The latter can occur either through using more products and services or referring friends and family. By understanding that each tool serves a different purpose and that each client at various stages in your relationship will require different things, you will see that a variety of communication methods work best.

78

Are there guidelines on what percentage of the total marketing budget should be allocated to existing clients versus that allocated to getting new clients?

The way to divide resources between marketing to existing clients and marketing to new clients depends on your marketing goals. If you are making a large effort to gain new clientele, the percentage of resources allocated may tip further toward reaching out to new clients than to current ones, although the general rule is to remember to butter your bread. In other words, pay the most attention to those patronizing your services, as they will likely generate a sizable portion of new clients anyway. Keep them coming back, using more services, agreeing to your recommendations, and, also important, spreading word-of-mouth referrals. This makes for healthier pets and a more profitable practice. Remember, retaining clients costs less than attracting new ones.

However, if you are a newer practice or have recently added a new veterinarian, you might be more focused on building a larger base of clients. Likewise, if you have added any new services, this might indicate more resources being spent on acquisition. With a new doctor, you have capacity to fill. With a new service, you may solidify relationships with those already patronizing your practice by virtue of this service, but you may also sway other pet owners to give you a try because of it. To attract new clients cost-effectively, take advantage of marketing a reason or rationale behind the outreach, such as "We've added another veterinarian to our team and expanded our hours—we are now welcoming patients on Sundays." For a new service, you might put out a message such as "Personalized nutrition plans now being offered for any overweight pet, including customized diets and weight loss programs." Both examples can and likely will also appeal to your current clients, but they may also tip the scales in your favor for some willing to consider a change.

79

Is paper marketing still worth the money?

Absolutely, but it depends on how you use it. One deterrent to printing materials is the perceived cost of printing and mailing. Today, however, great advances in the printing process have made full-color printing much more affordable. A good marketing agency likely has solid relationships with trusted printers who can work with you to select appropriate layout, size, paper stock, and even bulk mailing services to minimize cost and maximize impact.

When a client visits your hospital, it is good to offer a "take-with"—a brochure, pamphlet, or professionally designed handout of some sort. We all know that clients retain only a portion of what is told them at the clinic, and therefore having an opportunity to bring materials home can help them learn or retain more information, share it with family members or other pet caregivers, and keep your name and number ready and handy at any moment.

There are still many reasons to print materials, and, like any other communications medium, technology has evolved, so utilize today's preferred resources for the best printed products. You can even use recycled paper and soy-based inks to lessen your impact on the environment at the same time.

Is marketing of over-the-counter products worthwhile for a veterinary clinic?

You shouldn't spend a lot of time or money marketing OTC products outside of your practice. However, it is extremely important that you stock many of these products and take time to educate your clients about their importance. You may not make the margins you once did on parasite control, heartworm prevention, or even nonprescription NSAIDs because of online competition, but you are still the best source of information for any drug or nutritional supplement for pets. Surely you have a preference for some brands over others and it is your job to help guide your clients to make the best choice for their particular situation and pet. If you take a comprehensive approach to caring for the whole pet, then making sure you stock and sell all these types of products is not only good for business, it will ensure you are the most trustworthy source of information about the proper products for pets. Many practices have a preferred brand or two and a clear understanding of their quality. Enlighten your clients; they want you to make a recommendation.

There has been concern about the efficacy of drugs purchased over the Internet and the quality control process they may or may not undergo. This is a controversial topic, so it is always best to provide information to clients about prescription drugs and your perspective on the pluses and minuses of medication sources and nutritional products for their animals.

81

What is considered a successful return rate and return on investment for mailers such as Valpak?

Unfortunately, these types of mailers are not typically very cost-effective. In general, a mass mailing is considered effective if it yeilds a 2 percent return. A better approach is to target pet owners as opposed to just anyone in a particular zip code, as Valpak inserts do.

It would be more cost-effective to partner with an aligning business to do some cross-promotion. Perhaps the pet resort in town or the busy groomer down the street would like access to other pet owners, and vice versa. You could either promote the neighborhood service or produce a mailer that goes out to both mailing lists. This could work in several ways. For example, you might design something that an aligning business is willing to include in its next client mailing. Therefore, that business is not giving away its mailing list but instead providing an endorsement of your services. Either way, gaining access to more pet owners with an attractive offer or by indicating an association with a trusted vendor will help garner new business better than a general mailer does.

82

How can I determine the return on investment for Internet advertising?

Determining the return on investment for Internet advertising should be easy. Depending on where you are advertising, the site should be able to give you exact statistics on the clicks and site visits you have received over a specified period of time. One of the beauties of electronic advertising is that it is among the most measurable of all marketing efforts.

Aside from seeing the data on how many people have viewed or clicked your ad, you still need a goal regarding these new visits or viewers. You want a professionally developed site, as Internet ads are generally designed to drive traffic to your website. To evaluate the effectiveness of your site's capacity to convert visitors into clients, your site should be set up to capture statistics on visitors' surfing habits while they are on your site. After a designated period of time from the launch of each promotion or ad campaign, use these site statistics to analyze how well your site satisfied the needs of visitors and the sort of new business that resulted.

For instance, if your link delivered visitors to a specific page on your website and the abandon rate was high (those who left after seeing this page only), then you know that the message and design together did not satisfy the needs of your prospects. In contrast, if those who clicked on your ad spent an average of five minutes on the site visiting more pages, you have captured the attention of more people and can determine what they are interested in knowing about based on the pages they visited.

Keep in mind that some of your traffic may be current customers who are not showing up as new clients; however, you are clearly serving a need for them, as they have turned to you as their source of information. This further bonds them to you, but will not necessarily show up in the statistical information you are capturing. There are lots of factors to evaluate, and as always, working with a good marketing firm can help you make sense of the numbers. (Also see Question 83 for return on investment from websites.)

How do I figure out the return on investment on my website?

It is difficult to gauge a specific return on investment, but many tools can help you evaluate how your site is being used. Because your website is probably the single most frequently accessed area of information about your practice, it is vital that you devote time and attention to creating one that is professional, attractive, easy to navigate, and designed to make your clients' lives easier.

A knowledgeable Web development firm can help you get set up with Google Analytics, a free service that assists in tracking which pages on your site are accessed, how long visitors stay on your site, which page they leave from, and so on. In this way you can work with the developer to determine which areas of the site are working and which could use improvement to meet the needs of your clients.

These stats can and should be used to help you evaluate the effectiveness of other marketing initiatives. For instance, every time you send out an electronic newsletter, there should be links to your website for more information. You should see a corresponding spike in traffic to the site and specific pages for a period of time after the newsletters go out. By analyzing this information, you can learn a lot about your clients' interests, the topics you may want to expand upon in future communications, and so forth. You can also see how other types of programs are working.

Keep in mind that a website's purpose goes beyond generating income. Of more concern is the number of people who are not choosing you because of a poorly designed or unprofessional-looking site—something you can't measure. You will never regret putting time and energy into your online image because your site is doing most of the heavy lifting previously done by your staff. Give your website the investment it deserves and it will return your investment many times over.

84

How do I figure return on investment on new signage or building amenities?

Good signage is like an investment that keeps on giving. If you are on a main road and thousands of people see your sign every day, consider it the cost of a good billboard that you don't have to pay for month after month. If you have the liberty of designing a sign and not simply placing lettering in an office park or strip mall, be creative and make sure the sign has a design style similar to your logo and the interior of the practice. It can set the stage for what a visitor will find inside and serve as a good subtle introduction to your services. Keep it in good repair and, if possible, illuminate it. No sense in having your name out there only during daylight hours—use all 24 of them!

Building amenities are useful in fulfilling the experience part of a pet owner's visit. Anytime you can add to ambience as well as health care services for a greater perception of value, you will reap financial rewards. These are often unconscious takeaways for the client, so you will not see a direct correlation in return on investment, but suffice it to say, you want to offer the absolute best experience you can. This includes, for example, a clean parking lot, fresh flowers out front (weather permitting), soft lighting, refreshments, uplifting artwork, and attractive colors.

85

How do I figure out whether referral websites (Yelp, Insider Pages), Google (adwords, sponsored link), online yellow pages listings, or other online listings are worth the money?

If you pay for online placement, such as a sponsored link or yellow pages listing, the provider should be able to send reports with statistics on clicks received within a designated time frame. That is part of what you are buying.

You can always buy a trial period, such as 90 days, to see how the ad does for you. Work with the advertising vendor to determine realistic projections based on how other practices with similar demographics have fared. And take the time to create a compelling ad to capture the most attention. If you are going to try it out, execute it in the best way possible for a true test.

What happens once a visitor gets to your website is your responsibility, and if your Web developer has set you up with site analytics (Google Analytics is free), you can also evaluate the effectiveness of your site content and design, so make sure you invest properly here.

Of course, you should ask every person who enters your practice how they heard about you, or if they use your website and find it useful. Feedback from your clients is always valuable, so get in the habit of asking.

How do I measure my return on investment from an open house?

In order to determine your return on investment from an open house, you need to decide, before you throw the event, its purpose and goals. See Question 48 for more on open houses. In measuring success, consider the following, for example: How many people attended? What was the breakdown of current clients versus prospective clients in attendance? Did current clients learn something new about you? Did you schedule any appointments as a result? Did you sell any retail products? Did you gather email addresses to communicate with pet owners more efficiently? What types of questions were asked by pet owners? Did you provide educational materials along with token gifts? Did your staff actively engage in conversation and use the open house as an opportunity to develop a deeper relationship with clients? Did all veterinarians participate and introduce one another to clients often seen by an associate?

There are many ways to spell success with an open house. But you must know beforehand what you would like to accomplish and what role each member of your team should play in order to determine your level of success. In general, open houses take far more planning than expected to provide a truly exceptional experience. If you keep in mind that you want to deliver an "experience," you will incorporate more creative ideas in the process and are more apt to come away from the event exhilarated by the feedback.

87

What is the best way to market in a down economy?

The best way to market in a down economy is not to stop marketing. Study after study has been conducted comparing what happens to businesses that market through a recession with what happens to those who significantly slow down or stop. Those who continue to reach out to their target audiences always come out ahead after the recovery, and in nearly all cases, they gain market share as well.

A writer for *The New Yorker*, James Surowiecki, cites an example of how well the Post and Kellogg companies reacted to the Depression. Post did the intuitive thing: They cut expenses, including advertising. But Kellogg doubled its marketing budget, moved aggressively into radio ads, and heavily pushed its new cereal, Rice Krispies. This strategy paid off. By 1933, even as the economy tanked, Kellogg's profits had risen almost 30 percent, and it became what remains today the industry's dominant player. Surowiecki goes on to say: "Recession makes the strong stronger and the weak weaker. The strong can afford to keep investing while the weak have to devote all their energies to staying afloat. When the weak scale back on marketing, the campaigns of strong companies have a greater impact."

"How" to market during these economically challenging times is the question. The first line of defense is to improve customer service. Every practice complains that there is never enough time to train, so when times are slow, take advantage of the extra time and boost the skills of your staff. Training should emphasize value. Now more than ever, your clients need to understand what they are paying for (and why) in order to choose health care services for their pets. Focus on a few things you do well that are easy to communicate, are easy for the pet owner to understand, and generate profit. By providing continuing education in tough economic times, when you have little opportunity to make mistakes, you will have a better chance of getting it right the first time.

Double down on your current clients. Use the time to solidify your relationships with your client base, delivering an exceptional experience and potentially generating referrals.

Invest in growing market segments to get out ahead. If the competition has stopped performing a service for which you know there is a market, pick up the slack. Better yet, launch something new that you know is needed or underserved.

Finally, tidy up. Now is the time to refresh the practice—new paint, signage, artwork, whatever you can do to make the clinic experience more comfortable.

Are welcome postcards the best way to reach new move-ins in the vicinity of our hospital?

Welcome postcards are one way to reach new move-ins, but there are other ways to increase your reach as well. Consider working with other service businesses in the area to offer those new to the area a special introductory service. For instance, at the local doggy day care, groomer, dry cleaner, or strip mall, ask whether you can leave information on their counter or bulletin board welcoming new residents with a special. If those businesses happen to be clients of yours, you may even create a barter system whereby for every referred new client, they get something in exchange. Work with those in the community who may serve a similar clientele and thus might be interested in your practice or who would be looking for common services near their new home.

If you are in a more urban setting, consider contacting property management companies for pet-friendly apartments and condos to see whether you can either advertise in their newsletter or provide an incentive offering to new tenants.

Is a phone book ad still worthwhile, or would money be better spent on Internet yellow pages or a website?

The simple way to determine the usefulness of a phone book ad is to run a report in your practice management software system and see how many people over the last year found your practice through an ad in the telephone book. Probably few, if any. If you simply feel you must have a presence, then choose a basic listing with your name, address, and telephone number. Redirect any money you were spending on phone book advertising to the area that ranked highest on your report of sources of new clients. Invest in what is working, not in what used to work. (See also Question 75.)

If you are not accustomed to running reports with your practice management software, call your vendor for assistance. Many programs have built-in reporting mechanisms, or you can easily customize certain reports. Some programs even allow you to schedule reports to be run automatically on specified dates, providing a simple way to compare trends over a consistent time period. If you are planning to integrate a new software program in the near future, consider its reporting functions as one of the key criteria for determining usefulness. If information is going in, there should be a way to organize how it comes out, giving you the necessary tools to measure many different aspects of your business.

90

How long should I stay with a program (six weeks, six months, or one year) before I determine its effectiveness?

Measuring the effectiveness of a marketing effort is essential for determining future allocation of resources. Each type of program should be evaluated based on what is most appropriate for the desired goal. For instance, if you put out an advertisement that has a time-sensitive call to action (e.g., "Schedule an appointment by January 31 to receive a free bath"), and if you don't get good results during January, then you must modify the offer or divert resources elsewhere.

Advertising on a onetime basis does not typically generate good results unless there is a significant offering that creates a sense of urgency. Usually an ongoing effort is more effective and can succeed in both increased branding and generating new business.

Publicity and branding efforts are more difficult to measure and need to be considered as part of an overall long-term strategy to build awareness, develop a reputation, and become a positive and desired part of the community. These types of campaigns, in some form, should run for the life of your business.

The most important aspect of any campaign is to determine before the launch what your goals are and what time intervals you want to track. Then evaluate trends over these designated time frames to determine effectiveness.

91

What is the most effective marketing technique for current clients: postcard reminders, emails, phone calls?

The answer to this question depends how well you know your clientele. Take their pulse frequently. What will be most effective is whatever method each client prefers. It is therefore an excellent idea to have multiple methods and to ask each of your clients how he or she want to be notified. This doesn't mean you shouldn't reach out to them by other methods too, but that some form of customization is available to meet each client's preference.

You must also consider the cost of your team's time. Using an outsourced postcard and/or email reminder service takes little staff time. Telephone calls, however, take a lot of time. By tracking trends, which your vendor should be able to do, you may find that a certain percentage of clients respond after receiving a postcard reminder. If this is followed by an email reminder with a link for scheduling an appointment, another percentage may be captured. And finally, if you have enough personnel, try to reach out by telephone to those clients who have not responded to previous reminders to schedule an appointment.

Serving clients individually yet prudently not only will be appreciated, but will turn into loyalty. You should expect, however, that as technology evolves, so will your clients' communication preferences.

92

How effective is regular newspaper advertising (print and online versions)?

Newspaper advertising typically is quite expensive. However, smaller community papers with a narrower readership closer to your desired audience might be a good alternative. The longer the commitment (for instance, a one-year insertion order), the lower the per ad cost. When you advertise just a few times, the ads can be more costly.

Carefully review the media kit for a potential publication and make sure the readership demographics strongly skew in favor of the type of clientele you want to reach. If having a presence in one or more of these papers is something you want, rotate several ads and avoid placing the same one every week or month. You are looking to create awareness and hit on a need a reader may have. Varying the message in your ads will help you capture a larger audience, and one of these ads may just come at the right time with the right solution.

Sometimes these publications have bundled options so that you can advertise both online and in print for a package price, which can be a great deal.

Do It Now

Have your staff create a list of community publications they read or that they think your clientele reads so you can evaluate each one as an avenue to reach a larger audience.

Is local commercial advertising (on Cablevision, for example) worth the expense?

The answer to this question, as is often the case, depends on what you hope to accomplish by the exposure. For example, one specialty hospital had a very successful run of ads on cable TV during a large dog show. For the amount of slots they were given over a specified period of time to a specific audience, the hospital determined that the money spent hit the target in a professional manner and was seen by those most likely to choose specialty care. The dog show was a large, prestigious event full of tradition and attended by deeply devoted animal lovers. It was therefore something the hospital wanted to be associated with, and it met their criteria for the image they wanted to portray.

Many practices automatically decline more expensive marketing tactics, but if the exposure is worth the cost and the results are favorable, this expenditure may be worthwhile for your clinic.

In the following example, a practice has reached a broad-based audience at a cost that usually would be considered beyond budget. But when you note all the positive associations, you'll see why they signed on for several years. A 24/7 pet hospital chose to be the sponsor of a program featuring an adoptable pet at every minor league baseball game at the ballpark. Not only are they helping the community by encouraging pet adoption and showing the "dog of the day" during the seventh-inning stretch on the field, but they are reaching an entirely new audience in a fun environment and promoting their practice, in particular their emergency services. This has proven to be an excellent way to reach a large pet-owning population they did not have the ability to reach previously. Because the sponsorship is for the duration of the season, they see new faces at each game, have a presence on the team's website, and are involved in many of the team's media events. Don't be afraid to explore these types of partnerships, as the cost may prove to be entirely worthwhile.

How do I find the time to stay focused on whatever marketing we start?

As with any other desired change in behavior, it starts with a decision. It is a highly unusual business that is successful without marketing. In your case, it should be as important as the inventory on your shelves—something you wouldn't go a week without ordering. If you need help getting started and setting realistic goals, engage a good marketing agency to help you develop a plan, ideally one that understands the animal health care industry.

Once you've made the decision to invest in marketing, commit to the plan. Marketing without a plan (i.e., sending a marketing piece out on a whim or as a reaction to competition or the economy) is simply less effective and ultimately much more expensive. Once you have a specific plan, budget the resources, delegate tasks, schedule activities, and monitor the results. As you begin to see positive results, you will probably find it motivating to continue on this path.

As mentioned in several other answers in this book, get in the habit of running reports by using your electronic medical records. You probably do this already to track financial information for monitoring revenue and expenses, so look at marketing data at the same time. These reports will allow you to track relevant numbers before you launch a particular tactic. Watch for trends and adjust accordingly, so you will stay motivated and on track.

95

As a specialty practice manager, how do I market our services to the pet-owning public without offending the general practitioners we serve?

Marketing your own services without jeopardizing your relationship with the surrounding general practice community depends on the demographics of the area and how much competition you have, as well as the strength of your relationship with the general practitioners (GPs). Approaching direct-to-consumer marketing from the angle of education can be effective, so long as you explain the typical relationships among the GP, specialist, and pet owner.

Do not simply reach out to the general public and bypass your primary source of cases—the GP. This would be akin to competing with your largest customer. A direct analogy in the music industry is a record label selling through distributors but then deciding it can make more money selling directly to the public. Not surprisingly, the record stores will launch a rebellion. Your GPs are, in essence, your distributors. If you are going to overtly compete with the referring veterinarians (rDVMs), you will have problems. Competing with a client is typically a setup for disaster.

Do everything in your power to assure primary care veterinarians of your intentions to provide specialized care only and then return the cases as deemed appropriate for the medical condition. Then do as you say. Over time, you will win over a portion of this audience. For those you cannot convert, just know that at some point they will retire!

Until then, provide educational value and participate in charitable events where you can create awareness of your practice with the public, and continue to take the high road when it comes to explaining to pet owners how referral relationships work. If a handful of general practitioners won't comply, savvy pet owners will understand who is causing the roadblock.

What is the most cost-effective means of reaching the pet-owning population to market specialty veterinary services?

The most cost-effective means of reaching the pet-owning population to market specialty services is general practitioners, because a relationship with them means you have access to their hundreds of clients. This is probably not what you were expecting for an answer. It is likely that 90 percent or more of your cases are coming via referrals from primary care veterinarians. If this is the case, 90 percent of your marketing time and resources should be directed at satisfying the needs of your referring community. (The case for emergency services differs, as discussed below.)

If, however, you are not getting good results through the veterinarians, you might try two things: First, do a better job of working with the GPs, as there is clearly room for improvement. Second, be active with the pet-owners in your area. If you can serve the community through charitable causes and educational events, and potential clients can see you acting in service to the community, you will benefit on many levels. Use these opportunities to educate the public about how you work with primary care veterinarians, and if you meet individuals whose veterinarians have not made a referral, you can be sure they will take that complaint back to their vet. Your goal is to let them know you are there and that specialists can be an integral part of their pets' health care team.

If an emergency service is part of your referral practice, you should reach out directly to the public to make them aware of your location and 24-hour access. This does not mean you can or should preclude working with area veterinarians. In fact, working in tandem with area veterinarians can help you access hundreds if not thousands of pet owners. But not everyone sees the vet on a regular basis, and they may experience an emergency whereby you are the best resource. Therefore, advertise in places that have a strong pet owner readership. Partner with similar businesses to gain referrals, and provide them with magnets or brochures to give their clients. You must be where clients are, so find concentrated populations and go to them. If you are participating at a community pet expo or 5K run for charity, put your best foot forward by using a professional pop-up tent or display and offer well-designed materials and clever giveaways with your practice's name and contact information on them. And have the team dress like a team, including a big smile! Then go have fun meeting your potential new clients.

97

How do we convey that we are a specialty clinic with excellent client service before the client has arrived and interacted with staff (i.e., how do we market excellent client service)?

The best way to market client service is to be known for it. Anyone can say they take excellent care of clients and pets, but actually establishing that as your reputation is another matter. Of course, this takes time, but once you become known for it, other people will do some of your marketing for you. For instance, when a general practitioner refers a client to you, if the GP knows you are excellent at taking care of clients' needs, he or she may convey this as the main reason for the referral. Likewise, it is validating to have testimonials on your website and perhaps even printed materials that demonstrate clients' positive experiences at your referral practice. Keep in mind that if excellent client service is something you want to be known for, everything related to your brand needs to convey this message, from design to copy, photography, facility décor, and communication style.

The challenge is consistency. To be known for something, it must happen consistently with the entire team. Think of Nordstrom department store, which is known for its service. Service is part of the Nordstrom company's core values, and great time and effort are put into training their teams to deliver on this core promise. You must be ready to employ the same level of commitment and keep training, revisiting the concept, finding new ways to evolve, and getting even better. Reputations take time to build, but only a nanosecond to destroy. Guard yours carefully.

How do I best approach (if at all) that veterinarian who hasn't referred a case?

Relationships are complicated, be they marriage or business relationships. The direct, respectful approach works best in this scenario, as it does in personal relationships. An invitation to visit with you at your practice and meet your colleagues might be a good place to start. Remember that relationships take time to build and happen step by step. Express an interest in working together. Be genuinely interested in learning about the doctor and his or her practice.

If a veterinarian calls you periodically for advice or to discuss a case but does not refer any clients, then a different conversation is needed. You might say something like "Jim, I enjoy talking with you and you obviously feel we have something of value to offer in the way of expertise since you call periodically. But I'm curious to know why you never refer any cases. It sure sounds like some of your patients would benefit by our expertise (or technology, etc.). Could you share your thoughts about this?" Broach the subject. You have nothing to lose and potentially a referral source and health care partner to gain.

How do we compete against general practitioners without formal advanced training who advertise specialized services at lower prices than our referral hospital does?

There will always be clients who base decisions about their pet's care solely on price. If the risk is worth the savings to these individuals, you will be unlikely to persuade them to choose the superior care your practice offers. However, the way to be competitive is to clearly communicate the quality of care that pets receive from board-certified specialists formally trained in a particular procedure and who have successfully performed it hundreds of times. Be sure to focus on the positive attributes of the specialized training that diplomates have completed, the level of expertise they have achieved, and how rare it is to be one of a few hundred veterinarians to have this credential. Avoid mentioning credentials other doctors do not have. This is about what makes you and your practice most qualified to care for pets with specialized needs.

Include information on your website about your specialized training and anything else that sets your care and services apart from those of a practice that offers general wellness care. Help visitors to your site understand the benefits of higher-quality training, experience, expertise, facilities, equipment, technologies, and resources of board-certified specialists. This approach to your website establishes a platform for discussion, educates pet owners, and makes quality of care a tipping point for clients choosing a veterinarian to deal with their pet's special need.

If you are communicating with general practitioners, particularly those who receive formal schooling decades ago, it is important to provide information about your qualifications in a way that helps advance their level of understanding and familiarity with current best practices for specific conditions. Better yet, invite them to your practice to see and learn more about appropriate equipment and procedures. This will increase their base of knowledge and enable good discussion with their clients about the pros and cons of a service and help them make the best referral.

100

How do I get my staff doctors to establish better relationships with referring vets?

Referral medicine is just that, based on receiving cases from someone else who deems you to be worthy of the referral and a good reflection on them. So the key to motivating staff specialists to create and nurture relationships with referring veterinarians is to establish from the outset that their employment is contingent upon building business and that part of their responsibility as a doctor at your specialty practice is to generate referral relationships for the entire practice, not just their own cases. Include these responsibilities in clearly defined terms in the employment agreement so that the performance expectations are articulated in advance. Salary guarantees should be designed to motivate a new doctor to build business incrementally, with monetary rewards at each defined increase level. Thus, hire only those who are willing to take ownership of their employment and are willing to collaborate and act as partners to their associate specialists by working to introduce referring veterinarians (rDVMs) to their colleagues. This is the essence of specialty and referral medicine. Without this attitude of relationship building, education, and health care partnership, you are merely directing cases to another practice that truly lives by this philosophy. If it is not you, it will be your competition.

ⅲ➡ **Do It Now**

Schedule a time to review your doctor contracts for language regarding their responsibility to build referral relationships. If you find this section of the contract inadequate, consult your attorney to see how you might include this in the next contract.

101

What are some good marketing tools for referral practices that, whether internal or external marketing, are unique, fun, simple, and inexpensive?

Think outside of the box. If you are a referral practice and your goal is to service the general practitioners of your community, buy a bunch of practice-branded umbrellas, and the next time it rains, deliver them to nearby veterinary practices. You need to find creative ways that are unique, memorable, and serve a purpose to reach out to clients (rDVMs). A gesture like this shows that you care and are willing to take the time to be there for them, even if it means a bit of inconvenience, to demonstrate your commitment to the partnership.

Get to know your rDVMs, their spouses' or partners' names, how many children they have, where they went to vet school, and their hobbies, and then acknowledge specific milestones. A simple handwritten note will do. In fact, it's one of the most overlooked but cost-effective tools available. Often considered an old-school tactic, in today's busy world who wouldn't appreciate a note acknowledging a referral, a birthday, a child's graduation, or publication in a trade magazine? Keep good notes in your medical records database that include this personal information so you can quickly refresh before or during a call. Everyone on your team will then have access to it so they can use it as baseline information to more easily establish a relationship.

An overlooked area of outreach is staff of nearby referring clinics. These staff members are sometimes unsung heroes who rarely receive recognition. Even though the doctor typically is the one who chooses where to refer a client, staff can do a lot to support the referral. If you offer a discount on services to staff of referring clinics, make sure they know about it. If they are satisfied clients, they are certain to offer kind words when the doctor refers clients to your practice. Acknowledge the staff periodically by restocking your brochures, dropping off coffee and bagels, providing Valentine's treats, and so forth.

ⅢⅢ➡ **Do It Now**

If you do not have professionally designed, branded note cards, have them created, and order enough for every associate in your practice to write three per week for a year. Stay on top of this task by monitoring it to see what a difference it can make.

RESOURCES

Publications

Adamson, Allen P. *BrandSimple: How the Best Brands Keep It Simple and Succeed* (Palgrave Macmillan, 2006), with foreword by Sir Martin Sorrell.

American Animal Hospital Association, *AAHA Referral Guidelines*. Available at www.aahanet.org/PublicDocuments/AAHAReferralGuidelines.pdf.

Boss, Nan, DVM. *Educating Your Clients from A to Z: What to Say and How to Say It*, Second Edition (AAHA Press, 2011).

Chamblee, Justin, CPA, MAcc, and Max Reiboldt, CPA, *Financial Management of the Veterinary Practice* (AAHA Press, 2010).

Dilenschneider, Robert, and Maria Bartiromo. *The AMA Handbook of Public Relations* (American Management Association, 2010).

Drucker, Peter F. All books by this author, educator, leader, and strategist, known as the father of modern management and marketing.

Edelman, Richard, Christopher P.A. Komisarjevsky, Rich Jernstedt, et al. *The Art of Public Relations: CEOs from Edelman, Ruder Finn, Burson Marsteller & More on the Secrets to Landing New Clients, Developing Breakthrough . . . and Your Firm to Clients* (Inside the Minds) (Aspatore Books, 2001).

Gladwell, Malcolm. *The Tipping Point: How Little Things Can Make a Big Difference* (Little, Brown, 2000).

Gostick, Adrian, and Chester Elton, *The Carrot Principle: How the Best Managers Use Recognition to Engage Their People, Retain Talent, and Accelerate Performance* (Free Press, 2007).

Heinke, Marsha L., CPA, and John B. McCarthy. *Practice Made Perfect—A Guide to Veterinary Practice Management* (AAHA Press, 2001).

Humphries, Jim, DVM. "Using the Power of the Press to Grow Your Practice," in *Veterinary Practice News*, 2005. Available at www.veterinarypracticenews. com/web-exclusives/press-grow-practice.aspx.

LeBlanc, Mark. *Growing Your Business*, Second Edition (Expert Publishing, 2003).

Smith, Carin, DVM. *Client Satisfaction Pays—Quality Service for Practice Success*, Second Edition (AAHA Press, 2009).

Tumblin, Denise, CPA. "Growing a Veterinary Practice in a Bad Economy," in *Veterinary Economics*, September 1, 2009. Available at http://veterinary business.dvm360.com/.

RESOURCES

Websites

www.4act.com. Video library at Animal Care Technologies.

www.about.com. A great search source, especially http://advertising.about.com/od/smallbusinesscampaigns/u/smallbusiness.com

www.Allaboutbranding.com.

www.DVM360.com. DVM 360, published by Advanstar Communications.

www.magazine.com. Trends Magazine, published monthly by Audio-Tech, Inc.

www.marketingpower.com. American Marketing Association.

www.robfrankel.com. Rob Frankel, noted branding expert.

www.sethgodin.com. Seth Godin, noted author, brand strategist, and marketing pillar.

www.veterinarypracticenews.com. Veterinary Practice News, published monthly by BowTie News.

www.vetmedteam.com. Entire practice curriculum of VetMedTeam.

www.VetPartners.org.

www.vspn.org. Veterinary Support Personnel Network.

LIST OF CONTRIBUTORS

Akins, Michael, DVM, All Creatures Animal Hospital
Altena, Nancy, DVM, Companions Animal Hospital
Applegate, Katheryn E., DVM, Standale Veterinary Hospital PC
Barnes, Bruce, DVM, 4 Paws Animal Hospital
Bartus, Michelle, Valley Veterinary Service, Inc.
Becker, Deborah, VMD, Downingtown Animal Hospital
Beckett, Chip, Beckett and Associates Veterinary Services, LLC
Bess, Amy, DVM, Bellefonte Animal Clinic
Black, Tom, DVM, Crescenta Valley Veterinary Hospital
Blum Animal Hospital
Blumberg, Joel, DVM, Santa Rosa Veterinary Hospital
Brooks, Thomas G., Fox Valley Veterinary Clinic
Burgwardt, Melinda R., DVM, Broadway Veterinary Clinic, PC
Buzzetti, Tony, DVM, Companion Animal Medical Center
Canfield, Donald, Seattle Veterinary Associates
Chace, Paul A., DVM, Advanced Veterinary Care
Chase, Bruce, DVM, Chase Veterinary Clinic
Clarkston Animal Medical Center
Cole Stenson, Tamera, DVM, Lone Star Veterinary House Calls
Colmery, Ben H., III, Dixboro Veterinary Dental and Medical Center
Cornwall, Bryan M., DVM, Advanced PetCare of Oakland, P.C.
Correll, Kevin, Animal Medical Center, Trappe PA
Corrie, Sandra J., DVM, Akron Animal Hospital, P.C.
Crestview Veterinary Hospital
Cropper, Susan, DVM, Cropper Veterinary Service
Davies, Anna, DVM, MS, DACVIM, Crossroads Animal Hospital
Davis, Jessie, Director of Practice Development
Dee, James, DVM, Hollywood Animal Hospital
Derrick, Elbert, DVM, Glenwood Falls Animal Hospital
Detrick, Melissa, Honey Brook Animal Hospital
Dew, Mark, DVM, DABVP, Animal HealthCare Center

Doherty, Michael, DVM, Lacey Animal Clinic

Downes, Kim, Animal Hospital of Rowlett

Eckler, Kathy, DVM, Gull Lake Animal Hospital

Erickson, Kevin, Kulshan Veterinarian Hospital

Farrell, Peter W., DVM, The Burnt Hills Veterinary Hospital, PC

Faver, Cliff, DVM, Animal Health Services

Finkler, Mark, DVM, Roanoke Animal Hospital

Finnell, Glenn, DVM, South Orlando Animal Hospital

Foster, Steve, DVM, Foster Animal Hospital, P.A.

Gates, Melissa A., DVM, Cordova Veterinary Hospital

Gleason, Marguerite, The Carolinas Animal Hospital and Dental Clinic

Godwin, Jeff, DVM, Animal Medical Clinic

Good, Cheryl, Dearborn Family Pet Care

Gordon, Robert, DVM, Oakland Animal Hospital

Graham, Glynes, Patterson Dog and Cat Hospital, Inc.

Groverman, Frederick A., DVM, Cotati Small Animal Hospital

Gruss, Kathi, DVM, Earlysville Animal Hospital

Habermann, Ray, DVM, Foothills Veterinary Clinic

Hadland, David P., East Islip Veterinary Group and Shinnecock Animal Hospital

Hannam, Heather, Prince George Veterinary Hospital Ltd.

Hauser, Wendy, DVM, Coal Creek Veterinary Hospital

Hayden, Amanda, DVM, Centerville Animal Hospital

Hennessy, Katie, Heartland Animal Hospital

Henshaw, Richard, Great Falls Animal Hospital

Herman, Michael, DVM, Northern Valley Animal Clinic, Rochester, MN

Hibler, Steven, DVM, Cinco Ranch Veterinary Hospital

Hickey, Charles, Short Pump Animal Hospital

Hill, Kelly, Gulfshore Animal Hospital

Hosie, Suann, Vancouver Animal Emergency Clinic Ltd.

Hudyncia, JM, Towanda Creek Animal Hospital

Huntington, Ann, DVM, Suffield Veterinary Hospital

Ingram, Joe, Aldine Mail Route Animal Hospital

Isbell, Nancy, Belltowne Veterinary Center

Jackson, Lisa, Practice Manager, Stone Veterinary Hospital

Jeffery, Brian, DuPage Animal Hospital

Johnson, Christy, CVPM, PHR, Pampered Pet Health Center

Johnson, Jennifer F., VMD, Stoney Creek Veterinary Hospital

Johnson, Matt, CVT, Animal Care Hospital of Morris

Joyner, Mike, East Lake Veterinary Hospital

Kearse, Frank, DVM, Animals' Hospital of Levittown

Keeney, Susan, Siena Animal Hospital

Kellner, Bill, DVM, Ark Veterinary Hospital

Kendall, Grant, North Portland Veterinary Hospital

Kerr, David J., North Hill Animal Hospital

Kerstong, Tammy L., DVM, Companions Animal Clinic

Kessler, Ingrid J., DVM, Animal Urgent Care and Emergency
    Veterinary Hospital

Klinger, Michael D., DVM, Valley Veterinary Clinic

Koseki, Takashi, You-Kara Veterinary Clinic

Kuitu, John R., DVM, Great Plains Veterinary Clinic

Leslie, Marie, DVM, Caring Hands Animal Hospital

Levy, Gary T., DVM, DABVP, Lakeview Veterinary Hospital, Inc.

Litochleb, Catalina, Pacific Palisades Veterinary Center

Ludwikow, Kristen A., CVT, Canton Animal Hospital LLC

Luntz, Jeffrey, The Animal Medical Hospital of Belair Road

Mannix, Jack, DVM, San Juan Animal Hospital

Mattox, Diana, San Antonio Animal Hospital

McDonald, James W., DVM, Woodbridge Animal Hospital

McEwan, Ann, Carleton Place Veterinary Hospital

McInnis, Doug, DVM, West Ridge Animal Clinic

Mcpartlin, Marlene, Broadway Oaks Animal Hospital

Meisels, Lloyd S., DVM, Coral Springs Animal Hospital

Miller, James, DVM, Pet Medical Center—Chatoak

Mitchell, Deborah, DVM, MS, Knollwood Hospital for Pets

Mortimer, Randy, DVM, Quioccasin Veterinary Hospital

Moser, Karina, MA, Charlotte Street Animal Hospital

Myer, Paul, Hawthorne Animal Hospital

Nelson, Peter, DVM, Valley Veterinary Service, Inc.

Nichols, Cynthia, DVM, Parkview Veterinary Hospital

Nichols, Pam, DVM CCRP, Animal Care Center

Niebojeski, Felecia, DVM, Animal Hospital of Clinton

O'Hanlon, Kenneth, DVM, All Pets Medical Center

Ornelas, Leslie, Westside Animal Hospital

Pane, Bob, South Kendall Animal Clinic and Hospital

Parker, Deb, Kimberly Crest Veterinary Hospital

Patton, Sue, North Boulder Companion Animal Hospital

Peterein, Cheryl, Harwood Oaks Animal Clinic

Pierson Mason, Eloise, Peaks View Animal Hospital

Pitts, Kathy, Hospital Administrator, Animal Medical Center of Cumming

Plauche, Kristin, DVM, Lafayette Veterinary Care Center

Power, Peggy, Columbia Veterinary Hospital

Prevatt, William J., DVM, New Frontier Animal Medical Center

Pruyn, Minott, DVM, Pruyn Veterinary Hospital

Quinn, Gary J., VMD, Raritan Animal Hospital

Radding, Carolyn, VMD, Freeport Veterinary Hospital

Redford, Cliff, DVM, Wellington Vet Clinic

Reeves, Trevor, South Peace Animal Hospital

Ritter, Glen A., DVM, Riverside Animal Hospital LLC

Robinson, Steve, El Camino Veterinary Hospital

Rosene, David S., DVM, Shorewood Animal Hospital, SC

Rumble, Paul K., DVM, Pond Point Animal Hospital

Salinger, Elaine, DVM, White Ivie Pet Hospital

Salzsieder, Karl, Yelm Veterinary Hospital

Sargent, Brett, Front Range Veterinary Clinic

Sargent, Dwayne, Front Range Veterinary Clinic, Pc

Schaeberle, Thomas, VMD, Shiloh Veterinary Hospital

Schroeder, Fred, College Blvd Animal Hospital

Schroyer, Butch, DVM, Animal Care Clinic

Schwartz, Al, DVM, Moorpark Veterinary Hospital

Severidt, Dean, DVM CEO, Pet Doctors of America

Sheegog, Robert M., Jr., DVM, Onslow Animal Hospital

Sherman, Beverly, Parkcrest Veterinary Hospital

Smith, Albert, VMD, Charlottesville Veterinary Hospital

Smith, Carter B., Ellisville Veterinary Hospital

Smith, Cathi, DVM, Oak Park Veterinary Clinic

Smith, Willie, DVM, Willowrun Veterinary Hospital

Staley, E.C., DVM, MS, Staley's Veterinary Medical Clinic, PC

Stearman, William, DVM, Coppell Veterinary Hospital, P.A.

Stevenson, Tammy, Advanced Pet Care Clinic

Stucki, Heidi E., DVM, Shaver Road Animal Hospital

Sukhija, Aman, DVM, Atlantic Animal Hospitals

Takashima, Gregg K., DVM, The Parkway Veterinary Hospital

Tassinaro, Nicole, NorthStar VETS

Taul, Darren, Lancaster Veterinary Center

Tenorio, Kristin, Wauwatosa Veterinary Clinic

Trimmier, Erin, DVM, Ambassador Animal Hospital

Visser, David A., DVM, Roseland Animal Hospital and Center for Animal Health

Westfall, Mike, Hudson Road Animal Hospital PA

White McLean, Christy, The Animal Hospital of Waynesville

Widenmeyer, John C., DVM, Flowers Mill Veterinary Hospital Inc.

Willerton, Nancy, University Hills Animal Hospital

Wood, Willam, DVM, Pioneer Animal Hospital

Yankauskas, Paula J., VMD, Lamoille Valley Veterinary Services

ABOUT THE AUTHOR

Robin Brogdon, MA, received her Bachelor of Arts degree in cultural anthropology from the University of Michigan and her Master of Arts degree in organizational communication and marketing from Eastern Michigan University. For the past 25 years she has applied that knowledge through her work in business administration and marketing for a Big Ten university athletic department, a professional sports franchise, and a fast-growing media company, as well as a variety of management consulting engagements and leadership roles in specialty veterinary practices.

Robin has successfully taken companies through start-up, acquisition, and divestiture, with oversight and management of all aspects of the process. She has coordinated many building and relocation projects spanning multiple offices and cities, including the construction and opening of City of Angels Veterinary Specialty Center, a 30,000-square-foot comprehensive specialty hospital in Los Angeles. She helped lead the team of partners, specialists, and support staff through construction and operational start-up, including the development of a robust referral network. Meeting accelerated revenue goals in a competitive market was accomplished by creating and implementing a strategic marketing plan that concentrated on partnership with the referring veterinary community and incorporated continuing education and other key marketing elements.

In 2007, Robin launched BluePrints Veterinary Marketing Group, Inc., a full-service marketing agency devoted exclusively to serving businesses within the animal health care space. To accommodate a growing client base, BluePrints merged with Circa Healthcare in 2010. Circa is a well-established marketing, advertising, and promotion company that specializes in animal and human health care and has provided services in this marketplace for clients such as Intervet/Schering-Plough Animal Health, Boehringer Ingelheim Vetmedica, and Virbac.

Robin has lectured at numerous veterinary conferences, including AAHA, NAVC, VSIPP, ACVIM, and AVMA. She regularly contributes to industry trade publications and is a member of VetPartners, American Animal Hospital Association, Southern California Veterinary Medical Association, and Veterinary Emergency and Specialty Practice Association. She was recently elected to the Foundation Board of Directors of the American College of Veterinary Internal Medicine Foundation, and is the first nonveterinarian to hold this position.

Raised in suburban Baltimore, Robin relocated to southern California more than 20 years ago. She and her husband reside in Huntington Beach with their rescued, mixed-breed dogs, Libby and Maddie. In her free time, you can usually find Robin running at the beach or hiking the red-rock canyons of southern Utah.